D0594157

WITHDRAWN

ALSO BY THE AUTHOR

Crisis Real Estate Investing

HOW TO STOP FORECLOSURE

America's leading expert
tells you how to
save your home and
property

Hal Morris

*with an introduction
by Robert Irwin*

STATE LIBRARY OF OHIO
SEO Regional Library
Caldwell, Ohio 43724

BEAUFORT BOOKS, INC.
New York / Toronto

Copyright © 1983 by Hal Morris
All rights reserved. No part of this publication may be reproduced or transmitted in any form
or by any means, electronic or mechanical, including photocopy, recording, or any information storage and retrieval system now known or to be invented, without permission in writing
from the publisher, except by a reviewer who wishes to quote brief passages in connection
with a review written for inclusion in a magazine, newspaper, or broadcast.

Library of Congress Cataloging in Publication Data
Morris, Hal.
    How to stop foreclosure.
    1. Mortgage loans. 2. Housing—Finance.
3. Foreclosure. I. Title.
HG2040.15.M67   1983   332.7'22   82-24399
ISBN 0-8253-0146-7

Published in the United States by Beaufort Books, Inc., New York.
Published simultaneously in Canada by General Publishing Co. Limited

Printed in the U.S.A.   First Edition
10 9 8 7 6 5

85–35549

Contents

How to Stop Foreclosure

Preface
HOW TO STOP FORECLOSURE

AVONDALE, Pa.—Distraught over losing his house to foreclosure, a man held a magistrate and his wife at gunpoint for over five hours.

SPRINGFIELD, Colo.—Three hundred farmers protesting the foreclosure sale of a 320-acre farm tried to break down the Baca County Courthouse doors but were turned back by tear gas.

SAN DIEGO, Calif.—An entire city, Jacumba, located in San Diego County, went on the foreclosure auction block with an opening minimum bid of 1,353,000 dollars. (The city included 250 acres, a 65-room resort hotel, commercial buildings, and houses and had 400 residents.)

These are not made-up stories. They and others like them are actually happening. They bring to light the magnitude of the foreclosure problem that this country is facing.

I was not aware of how serious an issue foreclosures were until I appeared on the television shows, "A.M. San Francisco" and "P.B.S. Late Night." I discussed stopping foreclosure. The phone calls started coming in, and before it was over the stations reported they had received a record number of calls, with over 5,000 calls from people asking for specific kinds of help!

The problem, of course, is that the person facing foreclosure has had very little help at all. This was brought home to me when I took a television crew on location to a foreclosure auction where forty-seven different homes were being auctioned off through foreclosure (for my television show, "Money, Money, Money").

Both the television crew and I were shocked to see that there were only two people who showed up that day, and neither was there to bid on the houses. All the properties were lost to the lenders!

Across the country today more than a million properties are delinquent thirty days or more or in foreclosure, and the number grows each week. Homeowners, builders, investors, farmers, syndicators, owners of commercial property—no area of real estate has been untouched.

Yet, what can a person do?

The answer is a great deal. I wrote this book specifically to help the person facing foreclosure. In it I hope to give you an idea that will help you. Some ideas you may want to try; others you may not be willing to use. Overall, however, if you are facing foreclosure, you should find at least one (and probably many more) good alternatives here.

It is possible to stop foreclosure. This book will show you how to begin.

Note to the reader: This publication is intended to present the author's experiences and is being sold with the understanding that the author is not engaged in giving legal or other professional service. For legal problems it is suggested you consult with an attorney in your area.

The publisher and author specifically disclaim any personal liability for any loss or risk incurred as a consequence of any use, direct or indirect, of advice or information contained in this book.

Introduction:
WHY SO MANY PROPERTIES ARE IN FORECLOSURE

More people are facing foreclosure today than at any time since the Great Depression. What's worse is that their numbers are growing daily. The foreclosure rate, in fact, has reached epidemic proportions. It has gotten to the point where if we were facing a disease, the Surgeon General would have declared a national state of emergency.

Foreclosure to most people means loss. (Interestingly, in our current economy it often means loss for the lender as well as the borrower.) A family suddenly finds that it no longer has a home to live in, that it is literally going to be thrown out onto the street, losing the down payment and all the monthly payments it has already made on its home.

Foreclosure is a traumatic and costly experience, as anyone who has ever faced it will quickly testify. It is something to be avoided. Yet, as I've indicated, the number of foreclosures is increasing to what may soon become historic highs. Why? Why are there so many foreclosures today?

There are many reasons, all of which have come together to confront the homeowner in today's economy. Here's a list of five major reasons for foreclosure:

1. *Balloon payments.* During the good times of just a few years ago, many home *buyers* gave sellers "seconds," "thirds," or other junior mortgages as part of the sales price. (The buyers didn't have all the cash to buy, and because of high interest rates, they couldn't afford new mortgages, so they took over an existing low interest "first" and gave the seller a "second.")

The trouble is that those "seconds" almost always contained a balloon payment. They were for two to five years interest only. At the end of that time, the whole principal amount was due.

The idea was that at the end of the time, the borrower would refinance out. But high interest rates and tight money have made that virtually impossible for most people. Therefore, those big balloon mortgages now coming due are suddenly going into foreclosure at an alarming rate. In New York alone it has been estimated that by 1984, 1.6 billion dollars in balloon payments will come due. In California the figure is 3.9 billion dollars by 1985!

2. *High payments.* In the late seventies and early eighties, hundreds of thousands of people felt that real estate prices were going to continue skyrocketing upward indefinitely. After prices in many areas doubled or tripled between 1974 and 1980, these people felt that prices would double and redouble again. They believed that if they didn't buy and buy quickly, it would be too late for them. They would never have a chance to own their own home.

So they bought, often purchasing well beyond their means, hoping to either refinance out to a lower payment mortgage when interest rates dropped, or to sell for a profit and then use that money to purchase another home. But interest rates didn't drop. Housing prices dropped instead and the plan went awry.

Today savings and loan associations and banks report the highest rates of foreclosure on first mortgages since the Great Depression. Many banks report a *quadrupling* for first mortgage foreclosures between 1981 and 1982 alone and an equal increase expected for the next several years. One bank has over 1,000 properties taken back in foreclosure. People who got in over their heads and can't handle their monthly payments are bailing out.

3. *Poor farm prices.* In the farm belt—Iowa, Kansas, the Da-

kotas, and surrounding states—it has been estimated that fully fifty percent of farmers will be in foreclosure by the end of 1983. The reason—again, it's high interest rates, this time combined with bumper crops and recession-lowered prices. The farmers simply can't make enough money to pay for the loans they need to survive.

4. *Speculators*. They are another major cause of foreclosures today. Back when real estate was booming, anybody who could scratch together the down payment and the credit bought a second house. Many bought third, fourth, fifth, and more houses. The idea was to rent them out and then sell, once the price had jumped up again.

The problem, of course, is that the price didn't jump up again—rather the price of homes in most areas has fallen. Speculators usually faced with a high negative cash flow (paying out in mortgage, taxes, and insurance much more than they take in in rents) are bailing out. They are letting their rental houses go to foreclosure.

5. *Government decisions*. These decisions, finally, have tightened the noose around borrowers. The DelaQuesta decision and Garn-St. Germain bill in 1982 made it virtually impossible to assume many old low interest rate loans. That meant it was exceedingly difficult for people who wanted or were forced to sell their homes to make a sale. Buyers who couldn't assume old low interest rate loans had to come up either with cash or qualify for new high interest rate loans. Studies show that less than ten percent of all Americans can qualify for a *new* home loan. Less than *one* percent can pay cash.

These then are the big reasons why we are facing a foreclosure epidemic. These five factors, like fingers, are strangling homeowners and forcing them to lose their homes in numbers that most of us have never seen in our lifetimes.

But it should be understood that owners/borrowers are not the only ones who are suffering. In many cases sellers/lenders are suffering as well. It is a well-known truth that *foreclosure only works for lenders in good times*. In bad times foreclosure is the last thing a lender wants.

Lenders of mortgages are also in trouble. Savings and loan associations and banks have seen their "REO" or real estate owned portfolio (property taken through foreclosure) swell enormously. These properties do not provide the cash flow (from interest payments) that these institutional lenders need to survive. They can't resell in a down market with so many properties in foreclosure. The sheer volume of foreclosed properties is threatening the solvency of many large banks and savings and loans.

Individuals who loaned money on "seconds" to help sell their homes are in worse straits. Often they are not in a financial position to handle the costs of foreclosure. Many times they just lose their money as they helplessly watch the senior (first) mortgage foreclose.

Lenders troubles mean something special to the person facing foreclosure. They mean that *there has never been a better time for negotiating with lenders.* Lenders, whether they are private individuals (such as sellers of homes) or institutions (such as banks or savings and loan associations), don't want to foreclose on property. In fact, that's the *last* thing they want to do. If they foreclose and take the property back, then they are stuck with it. If you, the current owner, are holding onto it, then at least there's someone else working with them to help make the payments.

The borrower has a greater opportunity to negotiate with the lender in today's market than at any time in the past fifty years. It doesn't matter what's written in the loan documents. It doesn't matter that you, the borrower, are fully committed to make the monthly payments or fulfill the balloon payment. What matters is that if you can't perform, the lender's only option (in almost all cases) is to take the property back—and that's the last thing that nearly any lender wants to do.

In today's market, foreclosure to the lender means losing money. Therefore, lenders as never before are willing to overlook or even tear up the old mortgage agreement in an effort to reach a compromise that will allow you, the borrower, to keep your house and the lender to keep getting interest.

Don't give up if you're facing foreclosure. In the vast majority of cases foreclosure can be either avoided altogether or at least postponed for a long period of time.

In this book, Hal Morris gives you the tools you need to stop foreclosure. Read the material carefully. Try the techniques that apply to your situation. Act timely. But above all, don't despair. Help is on the way.

ROBERT IRWIN

Chapter One
WHEN FORECLOSURE THREATENS

"Foreclosure . . . to shut out, brake, or terminate. An ending of all rights of the mortgagor or his grantee."
"The spectre of the auctioneer stalks throughout the land, haunting debtors in city, town and country. . . . Next to life itself, a home is man's most prized possession."
         —*Newsweek*, vol. 1, no. 1 (17 February 1933)

Foreclosure never happens unexpectedly. Yet it is always a shock when it does occur. We know that we're behind in our payments (or that we haven't come up with a big balloon payment). We know that the lender is anxious because he or she's been sending us letters in the mail saying in effect, "Pay up . . . or else!"

But we simply haven't been able to pay. We've been sitting tight, hoping for the best. Then one fine morning when we've just about been able to put the whole problem in the furthest corner of our mind, when we feel that our whole life is ahead of us and opportunity is everywhere, it hits like a 500-pound bomb.

We walk out to the mailbox and there it is: a formal-looking letter from either an attorney, a title insurance company, or a trustee. Suddenly the whole problem with the house comes back to us with a vengeance. All at once we remember that "our" house really isn't ours. For practical purposes, it belongs to the bank.

With trepidation we take the letter and open it gingerly, hoping that just maybe if we handle it delicately, it will do the same for us. But instead it hits us hard. Inside is a legal notice, which very quickly tells us that we are now officially *"in default."*

The notice probably looks something like the one on the facing page if we live anywhere other than the East Coast.

If we live in parts of the East Coast, New York for example, the notice might look like this:

> Dear Mortgagor [this means you, the borrower]:
> You have failed to make your monthly payment of $850, which was due on the first day of January. As a consequence, the mortgagee [the lender] does hereby declare the entire mortgage indebtedness due and payable and formal demand is made upon you for the principal balance of $65,000 together with interest of $2,100. The total amount you now owe is $67,100 and demand is hereby made for immediate payment.
>
> Sincerely,
>
> The Mortgagee

When our hands stop shaking, we discover that we are full of questions. Does this mean that we lose our house? According to the letter (or the default notice) we owe a horrendous amount of money, which we haven't a chance in the world of coming up with. Do we owe that money regardless of whether or not we lose our house? Can we make a partial payment, say last month's mortgage payment, and somehow make it all right again? Is there any way we can get more *time*? What should we do?

Obviously the thing for us not to do is panic.

Next we need to sit down, have a cup of tea or coffee, and think about something pleasant. Finally we need to get some perspective on what that letter really is and what it means to us.

Assuming we've had our tea and are calm, let's keep two very important things in mind:

    1. Foreclosure takes time (we're only at the start here).

    2. Foreclosure involves documents (such as the notice we've just received).

As we'll see, there are many ways to delay or stop foreclosure. For

RECORDING REQUESTED BY

AND WHEN RECORDED MAIL TO

NAME
STREET
ADDRESS
CITY &
STATE

Attn:

REFERENCE NUMBER

IMPORTANT NOTICE

IF YOUR PROPERTY IS IN FORECLOSURE BECAUSE YOU ARE BEHIND IN YOUR PAYMENTS, IT MAY BE SOLD WITHOUT ANY COURT ACTION, and you may have the legal right to bring your account in good standing by paying all of your past due payments plus permitted costs and expenses within three months from the date this Notice of Default was recorded.

This amount is $_____ as of _____, and will increase until your account becomes current. You may not have to pay the entire unpaid portion of your account, even though full payment was demanded, but you must pay the amount stated above. After three months from the date of recordation of this document (which date of recordation appears hereon), unless the obligation being foreclosed upon permits a longer period, you have only the legal right to stop the foreclosure by paying the entire amount demanded by your creditor. To find out the amount you must pay, or to arrange for payment to stop the foreclosure, or if your property is in foreclosure for any other reason, contact:

_____

_____

_____

If you have any questions, you should contact a lawyer or the government agency which may have insured your loan.

Remember, YOU MAY LOSE LEGAL RIGHTS IF YOU DO NOT TAKE PROMPT ACTION.

THE FOLLOWING COPY OF "NOTICE", THE ORIGINAL OF WHICH WAS FILED FOR RECORD
ON _____ IN THE OFFICE OF _____ COUNTY.
_____ THE RECORDER OF _____ CALIFORNIA.
IS SENT TO YOU INASMUCH AS AN EXAMINATION OF THE TITLE TO SAID TRUST PROPERTY
SHOWS YOU MAY HAVE AN INTEREST IN THE TRUSTEE'S SALE PROCEEDINGS.

NOTICE OF DEFAULT

NOTICE IS HEREBY GIVEN: THAT_____

_____is duly appointed Trustee under a Deed of Trust

dated   executed by

as Trustor, to secure certain obligations

in favor of

, as beneficiary

recorded   , as instru-   , in   , page   , of Official Records
                  ment no.   book   in the Office of the
Recorder of   County, California, describing land
therein as:

including   note   for the   sum of $ said obligations

that a breach of, and default in, the obligations for which such Deed of Trust is security has accurred in that payment has not been made of:

that by reason thereof, the present beneficiary under such Deed of Trust has deposited with said duly appointed Trustee, such Deed of Trust and all documents evidencing obligations secured thereby, and the undersigned does hereby declare all sums secured thereby immediately due and payable and does hereby elect to cause the trust property to be sold to satisfy the obligations secured thereby.

_____

_____

Dated_____   _____

FORM F-2 MPS

NOTICE OF DEFAULT

now we need to start with the fact that in the early stages there are two basic ways to stop foreclosure—stop the clock, or challenge the documents. We'll learn how to do both, but before we can do that we have to have some idea of what's happening and where we are in the process. Let's get back to that letter. What is the letter telling us?

The first thing we should understand is that the letter is starting a clock. A notice of default is not a completed foreclosure. A foreclosure is a process that takes time. The notice or letter is just the first step. It is the beginning of the procedure that *could* but not necessarily *will* end up in the loss of our home. It is notifying us that the foreclosure procedure has started and that now the ball is in our court.

The second thing we should look at is the word accelerated, which is in the letter and is implied in the notice of default form if swift action is not taken. Accelerated means that the rate of payback of the mortgage has been dramatically increased. Instead of having 360 monthly payments of 850 dollars left in which to pay off the mortgage, we now have only one payment of 67,100 dollars including interest left. Accelerated means that the lender is telling us he or she now wants *all* the money at once. (But that doesn't necessarily mean he or she's entitled to it, as we'll soon see.)

Finally, we should understand that a notice of default or letter of acceleration doesn't get sent to us for no reason. The only reason it gets sent is because either we aren't making our monthly payments or haven't made a balloon payment or lived up to another condition of our loan. We only get this document when we haven't fulfilled our signed-and-agreed-upon obligations under the mortgage.

If we have made all our monthly payments, if there was no balloon due, or if we paid it and we get this letter, we should immediately get on the phone to the lender and *demand* both an explanation and a satisfaction of default. (This is another notice, statement, or letter that clears up the matter of the first.)

WHY SECOND MORTGAGES FORECLOSE FIRST

Let's assume we haven't made several payments and that's the reason for the notice of default. We know why we got it. Now what happens?

The foreclosure procedure takes time. It doesn't happen over-

RECORDING REQUESTED BY

AND WHEN RECORDED MAIL TO

NAME
STREET ADDRESS
CITY & STATE

Attn:

REFERENCE NUMBER

NOTICE OF RESCISSION

NOTICE WAS RECORDED ON		IN THE OFFICE OF THE RECORDER OF
		COUNTY, CALIFORNIA,
DOC. NO.	IN BOOK	PAGE
		OF OFFICIAL RECORDS;

whereas, _____ is duly appointed Trustee under a Deed of Trust

executed by

dated

in favor of

recorded   as instru-   in   , as beneficiary
Recorder of   ment no.   book   page   , of Official Records
therein as: in the Office of the
                                                           County, California, describing land

and that:

On the day and in the book and page set forth above a Notice of Default was recorded.

Notice is now given that said Notice of Default is hereby rescinded, cancelled, and withdrawn. It is understood, however, that this Notice of Rescission shall not in any manner be construed as waiving or affecting any breach or default — past, present, or future, under said Deed of Trust or as impairing any right or remedy thereunder, but it is, and shall be deemed to be, only an election, without prejudice, not to cause a sale to be made pursuant to said notice, and shall in nowise jeopardize or impair any right, remedy, or privilege of the Beneficiary and/or the Trustee, under said Deed of Trust nor modify nor alter in any respect any of the terms, covenants, conditions thereof, and said Deed of Trust and all obligations secured thereby are hereby reinstated and shall be and remain in force and affect the same as if said Notice of Default had not been made and given.

Dated _____

FORM F-2 MPS

SATISFACTION OF DEFAULT NOTICE

night. The time it takes varies from state to state. The laws governing foreclosure differ, depending on what state you reside in.

Since we can't possibly cover all the states' procedures, we'll cover the two primary procedures used in two of the largest real estate markets: California and New York. We'll begin with California and the assumption that we have a first mortgage and a second mortgage on our property and that the notice of default is from the lender on the second mortgage. Perhaps our first question will be:

"If I have a 'first' and a 'second,' why is only the 'second' starting foreclosure?"

The answer has to do with the way payment is made to mortgage holders in the event of foreclosure. Briefly, if a property is sold in a foreclosure sale, the holder of the first mortgage is entitled to all the proceeds up to the amount of indebtedness of the "first." If the "first" is for 50,000 dollars and the house is sold for 51,000 dollars, the holder of the "first" gets the first 50,000 dollars (hence the name "first").

The holder of the "second" is allowed all the money left up to the value of the "second," after the "first" is paid off. If the "second" is for 5,000 dollars and the house sells for 51,000 dollars, the holder of the "second" gets only 1,000 dollars (that's all that's left after the "first" for 50,000 dollars has been paid off.) If there were a third mortgage, that lender would get nothing.

We also need to know that at a foreclosure sale all bids for the house are in cash *except* for those of the lenders, who may bid the value of their mortgage.

Now we can determine why a second mortgage holder will start foreclosure. The reason is that if we don't make payments and the first mortgage holder starts the procedure, at a foreclosure sale the holder of the "first" is going to bid the full amount of his or her mortgage, in this case, 50,000 dollars. If there are no other bidders, which is frequently the case, the house will be sold for that amount. This means the second mortgage holder *will get nothing*.

To prevent this from happening, when we stop making payments, the holder of the second mortgage will do two things. First, he or she will start making direct payments to the first mortgage holder, thereby preventing the first mortgage holder from foreclosing and costing the second mortgage holder his or her mortgage money. Second, as provided in his or her document, the second mortgage holder will add the payments he or she's making to the first mortgage holder onto the amount of the second mortgage and start foreclosure of the second mortgage.

At a foreclosure sale of a "second" with the "first" not foreclosing, what is sold is only the amount of the "second," in this case 5,000 dollars. The buyer purchases the property subject to the existing "first." The first mortgage holder's position is always protected (being first in line).

At the sale the holder of the "second" bids 5,000 dollars (the amount of the note). Assuming there are no other bidders, he or she takes title to the property subject to the existing "first" of 50,000 dollars.

Notice that by foreclosing and keeping up the payments on the "first," the holder of the "second" is able to protect his or her interest. By letting the "first" foreclose, the second mortgage holder would probably lose all his or her money.

This is why when we have more than one mortgage on a property, the holder of the most junior mortgage is usually the one to foreclose first.

TRUST DEED FORECLOSURE PROCEDURE

SECURITY DEVICES IN THE FIFTY STATES

Many states use mortgage and deed of trust. Below is listed the most common form used in each state. The states listed as both are either equally divided or usage is based upon the tradition of that particular region of the state.

SECURITY DEVICES

AL	Mortgage	HI	Mortgage
AK	Deed of Trust	ID	Deed of Trust
AZ	Deed of Trust	IL	Deed of Trust
AR	Both	IN	Mortgage
CA	Deed of Trust	IA	Mortgage
CO	Deed of Trust	KS	Mortgage
CT	Mortgage	KY	Both
DE	Mortgage	LA	Mortgage
FL	Mortgage	ME	Mortgage
GA	Mortgage	MD	Both

MA	Mortgage	OK	Mortgage
MI	Mortgage	OR	Deed of Trust
MN	Mortgage	PA	Mortgage
MS	Deed of Trust	RI	Mortgage
MO	Deed of Trust	SC	Mortgage
MT	Deed of Trust	SD	Mortgage
NE	Deed of Trust	TN	Deed of Trust
NV	Deed of Trust	TX	Deed of Trust
NH	Mortgage	UT	Deed of Trust
NJ	Mortgage	VT	Mortgage
NM	Deed of Trust	WA	Deed of Trust
NY	Mortgage	WV	Deed of Trust
NC	Deed of Trust	WI	Mortgage
ND	Mortgage	WY	Mortgage
OH	Mortgage		

Now let's get right to the procedure. We have been using the term mortgage, which is generic. In California and many other states a mortgage as a specific lending instrument is almost never used. In its place we have a trust deed. (We'll discuss the mortgage when we talk about New York.)

There are two parts to a trust deed. First of all there is the deed of trust itself. The trust deed is what I call the "what if" document. If payments aren't made, then there can be a foreclosure without going to court. Secondly there is the note that contains the obligation to pay back the money lent us. This is the evidence of indebtedness.

To understand why there are two documents we have first to understand that there are *three* parties to a trust deed:

Beneficiary (lender)

Trustor (borrower)

Trustee (stakeholder)

The beneficiary is the lender, the trustor, the borrower. But what is the trustee?

The trustee is an independent third party, often a title, escrow, or trust company specially set up to act as this party. When we (trustor) borrow money from a beneficiary (lender), we sign a deed (called the trust deed) to the trustee. This deed empowers the trustee to sell the property if we fail to meet our loan obligations.

We also, however, sign a second document, which is a note we

RECORDING REQUESTED BY

AND WHEN RECORDED MAIL TO

Name
Street Address
City & State

———— SPACE ABOVE THIS LINE FOR RECORDER'S USE ————

SHORT FORM DEED OF TRUST AND ASSIGNMENT OF RENTS (INDIVIDUAL)

A.P.N._____

This Deed of Trust, made this _____ day of _____ , _____ , between

_____ , herein called TRUSTOR,

whose address is _____

(number and street)　　　(city)　　　(state)　　　(zip)

_____ , a California corporation, herein called TRUSTEE, and

_____ , herein called BENEFICIARY,

Witnesseth: That Trustor IRREVOCABLY GRANTS, TRANSFERS AND ASSIGNS to TRUSTEE IN TRUST, WITH POWER OF SALE, that property in _____ County, California, described as:

TOGETHER WITH the rents, issues and profits thereof, SUBJECT, HOWEVER, to the right, power and authority given to and conferred upon Beneficiary by paragraph (10) of the provisions incorporated herein by reference to collect and apply such rents, issues and profits.

For the Purpose of Securing: 1. Performance of each agreement of Trustor incorporated by reference or contained herein. 2. Payment of the indebtedness evidenced by one promissory note of even date herewith, and any extension or renewal thereof, in the principal sum of $_____ executed by Trustor in favor of Beneficiary or order. 3. Payment of such further sums as the then record owner of said property hereafter may borrow from Beneficiary, when evidenced by another note (or notes) reciting it is so secured.

To Protect the Security of This Deed of Trust, Trustor Agrees: By the execution and delivery of this Deed of Trust and the note secured hereby, that provisions (1) to (14), inclusive, of the fictitious deed of trust recorded in Santa Barbara County and Sonoma County October 18, 1961, and in all other counties October 23, 1961, in the book and at the page of Official Records in the office of the county recorder of the county where said property is located, noted below opposite the name of such county, viz.:

COUNTY	BOOK	PAGE	COUNTY	BOOK	PAGE	COUNTY	BOOK	PAGE	COUNTY	BOOK	PAGE
Alameda	435	684	Kings	792	833	Placer	895	301	Sierra	29	335
Alpine	1	250	Lake	362	39	Plumas	151	5	Siskiyou	468	181
Amador	104	348	Lassen	171	471	Riverside	3005	523	Solano	1105	182
Butte	1145	1	Los Angeles	T2055	899	Sacramento	4331	62	Sonoma	1851	689
Calaveras	145	152	Madera	810	170	San Benito	271	383	Stanislaus	1715	456
Colusa	296	617	Marin	1508	339	San Bernardino	5567	61	Sutter	572	297
Contra Costa	3978	47	Mariposa	77	292	San Francisco	A332	905	Tehama	401	289
Del Norte	78	414	Mendocino	579	530	San Joaquin	2470	311	Trinity	93	366
El Dorado	568	456	Merced	1547	538	San Luis Obispo	1151	12	Tulare	2294	275
Fresno	4626	572	Modoc	184	851	San Mateo	4078	420	Tuolumne	135	47
Glenn	422	184	Mono	52	429	Santa Barbara	1878	860	Ventura	2062	386
Humboldt	657	527	Monterey	2194	538	Santa Clara	5336	341	Yolo	653	245
Imperial	1091	501	Napa	639	86	Santa Cruz	1431	494	Yuba	334	486
Inyo	147	598	Nevada	305	320	Shasta	684	528			
Kern	3427	60	Orange	5889	611	San Diego	Series 2 Book 1961, Page 183887				

(which provisions, identical in all counties, are printed on the reverse hereof) hereby are adopted and incorporated herein and made a part hereof as fully as though set forth herein at length; that he will observe and perform said provisions; and that the references to property, obligations, and parties in said provisions shall be construed to refer to the property, obligations, and parties set forth in this Deed of Trust.

The undersigned Trustor requests that a copy of any Notice of Default and of any Notice of Sale hereunder be mailed to him at his address hereinbefore set forth.

STATE OF CALIFORNIA,　　} SS.

COUNTY OF_____

On_____before me, the undersigned, a Notary Public in and for said State, personally appeared

_____

_____ , known to me to be the person___ whose name_____subscribed to the within instrument and acknowledged that_____executed the same.

WITNESS my hand and official seal.

Signature_____

Signature of Trustor

_____

_____

_____

Title Order No._____

Escrow or Loan No._____

(This area for official notarial seal)

TO 1939 CA(8-74) (OPEN END)

TRUST DEED

—— DO NOT RECORD ——

The following is a copy of provisions (1) to (14), inclusive, of the fictitious deed of trust, recorded in each county in California, as stated in the foregoing Deed of Trust and incorporated by reference in said Deed of Trust as being a part thereof as if set forth at length therein.

To Protect the Security of This Deed of Trust, Trustor Agrees:

(1) To keep said property in good condition and repair; not to remove or demolish any building thereon; to complete or restore promptly and in good and workmanlike manner any building which may be constructed, damaged or destroyed thereon and to pay when due all claims for labor performed and materials furnished therefor; to comply with all laws affecting said property or requiring any alterations or improvements to be made thereon; not to commit or permit waste thereof; not to commit, suffer or permit any act upon said property in violation of law; to cultivate, irrigate, fertilize, fumigate, prune and do all other acts which from the character or use of said property may be reasonably necessary, the specific enumerations herein not excluding the general.

(2) To provide, maintain and deliver to Beneficiary fire insurance satisfactory to and with loss payable to Beneficiary. The amount collected under any fire or other insurance policy may be applied by Beneficiary upon indebtedness secured hereby and in such order as Beneficiary may determine, or at option of Beneficiary the entire amount so collected or any part thereof may be released to Trustor. Such application or release shall not cure or waive any default or notice of default hereunder or invalidate any act done pursuant to such notice.

(3) To appear in and defend any action or proceeding purporting to affect the security hereof or the rights or powers of Beneficiary or Trustee; and to pay all costs and expenses, including cost of evidence of title and attorney's fees in a reasonable sum, in any such action or proceeding in which Beneficiary or Trustee may appear, and in any suit brought by Beneficiary to foreclose this Deed.

(4) To pay: at least ten days before delinquency all taxes and assessments affecting said property, including assessments on appurtenant water stock; when due, all incumbrances, charges and liens, with interest, on said property or any part thereof, which appear to be prior or superior hereto; all costs, fees and expenses of this Trust.

Should Trustor fail to make any payment or to do any act as herein provided, then Beneficiary or Trustee, but without obligation so to do and without notice to or demand upon Trustor and without releasing Trustor from any obligation hereof, may: make or do the same in such manner and to such extent as either may deem necessary to protect the security hereof, Beneficiary or Trustee being authorized to enter upon said property for such purposes; appear in and defend any action or proceeding purporting to affect the security hereof or the rights or powers of Beneficiary or Trustee; pay, purchase, contest or compromise any incumbrance, charge or lien which in the judgment of either appears to be prior or superior hereto; and, in exercising any such powers, pay necessary expenses, employ counsel and pay his reasonable fees.

(5) To pay immediately and without demand all sums so expended by Beneficiary or Trustee, with interest from date of expenditure at the amount allowed by law in effect at the date hereof, and to pay for any statement provided for by law in effect at the date hereof regarding the obligation secured hereby any amount demanded by the Beneficiary not to exceed the maximum allowed by law at the time when said statement is demanded.

(6) That any award of damages in connection with any condemnation for public use of, or injury to said property or any part thereof is hereby assigned and shall be paid to Beneficiary who may apply or release such moneys received by him in the same manner and with the same effect as above provided for disposition of proceeds of fire or other insurance.

(7) That by accepting payment of any sum secured hereby after its due date, Beneficiary does not waive his right either to require prompt payment when due of all other sums so secured or to declare default for failure so to pay.

(8) That at any time or from time to time, without liability therefor and without notice, upon written request of Beneficiary and presentation of this Deed and said note for endorsement, and without affecting the personal liability of any person for payment of the indebtedness secured hereby, Trustee may: reconvey any part of said property; consent to the making of any map or plat thereof; join in granting any easement thereon; or join in any extension agreement or any agreement subordinating the lien or charge hereof.

(9) That upon written request of Beneficiary stating that all sums secured hereby have been paid, and upon surrender of this Deed and said note to Trustee for cancellation and retention and upon payment of its fees, Trustee shall reconvey, without warranty, the property then held hereunder. The recitals in such reconveyance of any matters or facts shall be conclusive proof of the truthfulness thereof. The grantee in such reconveyance may be described as "the person or persons legally entitled thereto." Five years after issuance of such full reconveyance, Trustee may destroy said note and this Deed (unless directed in such request to retain them).

(10) That as additional security, Trustor hereby gives to and confers upon Beneficiary the right, power and authority, during the continuance of these Trusts, to collect the rents, issues and profits of said property, reserving unto Trustor the right, prior to any default by Trustor in payment of any indebtedness secured hereby or in performance of any agreement hereunder, to collect and retain such rents, issues and profits as they become due and payable. Upon any such default, Beneficiary may at any time without notice, either in person, by agent, or by a receiver to be appointed by a court, and without regard to the adequacy of any security for the indebtedness hereby secured, enter upon and take possession of said property or any part thereof, in his own name sue for or otherwise collect such rents, issues and profits, including those past due and unpaid, and apply the same, less costs and expenses of operation and collection, including reasonable attorney's fees, upon any indebtedness secured hereby, and in such order as Beneficiary may determine. The entering upon and taking possession of said property, the collection of such rents, issues and profits and the application thereof as aforesaid, shall not cure or waive any default or notice of default hereunder or invalidate any act done pursuant to such notice.

(11) That upon default by Trustor in payment of any indebtedness secured hereby or in performance of any agreement hereunder, Beneficiary may declare all sums secured hereby immediately due and payable by delivery to Trustee of written declaration of default and demand for sale and of written notice of default and of election to cause to be sold said property, which notice Trustee shall cause to be filed for record. Beneficiary also shall deposit with Trustee this Deed, said note and all documents evidencing expenditures secured hereby.

After the lapse of such time as may then be required by law following the recordation of said notice of default, and notice of sale having been given as then required by law, Trustee, without demand on Trustor, shall sell said property at the time and place fixed by it in said notice of sale, either as a whole or in separate parcels, and in such order as it may determine, at public auction to the highest bidder for cash in lawful money of the United States, payable at time of sale. Trustee may postpone sale of all or any portion of said property by public announcement at such time and place of sale, and from time to time thereafter may postpone such sale by public announcement at the time fixed by the preceding postponement. Trustee shall deliver to such purchaser its deed conveying the property so sold, but without any covenant or warranty, express or implied. The recitals in such deed of any matters or facts shall be conclusive proof of the truthfulness thereof. Any person, including Trustor, Trustee, or Beneficiary as hereinafter defined, may purchase at such sale.

After deducting all costs, fees and expenses of Trustee and of this Trust, including cost of evidence of title in connection with sale, Trustee shall apply the proceeds of sale to payment of: all sums expended under the terms hereof, not then repaid, with accrued interest at the amount allowed by law in effect at the date hereof; all other sums then secured hereby; and the remainder, if any, to the person or persons legally entitled thereto.

(12) Beneficiary, or any successor in ownership of any indebtedness secured hereby, may from time to time, by instrument in writing, substitute a successor or successors to any Trustee named herein or acting hereunder, which instrument, executed by the Beneficiary and duly acknowledged and recorded in the office of the recorder of the county or counties where said property is situated, shall be conclusive proof of proper substitution of such successor Trustee or Trustees, who shall, without conveyance from the Trustee predecessor, succeed to all its title, estate, rights, powers and duties. Said instrument must contain the name of the original Trustor, Trustee and Beneficiary hereunder, the book and page where this Deed is recorded and the name and address of the new Trustee.

(13) That this Deed applies to, inures to the benefit of, and binds all parties hereto, their heirs, legatees, devisees, administrators, executors, successors and assigns. The term Beneficiary shall mean the owner and holder, including pledgees, of the note secured hereby, whether or not named as Beneficiary herein. In this Deed, whenever the context so requires, the masculine gender includes the feminine and/or neuter, and the singular number includes the plural.

(14) That Trustee accepts this Trust when this Deed, duly executed and acknowledged, is made a public record as provided by law. Trustee is not obligated to notify any party hereto of pending sale under any other Deed of Trust or of any action or proceeding in which Trustor, Beneficiary or Trustee shall be a party unless brought by Trustee.

—— DO NOT RECORD ——

REQUEST FOR FULL RECONVEYANCE

To be used only when note has been paid.

To _____ Dated_____

The undersigned is the legal owner and holder of all indebtedness secured by the within Deed of Trust. All sums secured by said Deed of Trust have been fully paid and satisfied; and you are hereby requested and directed, on payment to you of any sums owing to you under the terms of said Deed of Trust, to cancel all evidences of indebtedness, secured by said Deed of Trust, delivered to you herewith together with said Deed of Trust, and to reconvey, without warranty, to the parties designated by the terms of said Deed of Trust, the estate now held by you under the same.

MAIL RECONVEYANCE TO:

_____

_____

_____

By _____

By _____

Do not lose or destroy this Deed of Trust OR THE NOTE which it secures. Both must be delivered to the Trustee for cancellation before reconveyance will be made.

TRUST DEED

Short Form Deed of Trust

WITH POWER OF SALE

(INDIVIDUAL)

AS TRUSTEE

DO NOT DESTROY THIS ORIGINAL NOTE: When paid, said original note, together with the Deed of Trust securing same, must be surrendered to Trustee for cancellation and retention before reconveyance will be made.

NOTE SECURED BY DEED OF TRUST
(INSTALLMENT — INTEREST INCLUDED)

$ _____, California,_____, 19____

In installments as herein stated, for value received, I/we, jointly and severally, promise to pay to_____ _____

_____

_____

or order, at_____the sum of

_____DOLLARS

with interest from_____on unpaid

principal at the rate of_____per cent per annum; principal and interest payable in installments of_____

_____DOLLARS

or more on the_____day of each_____month, beginning on the_____

day of_____, 19____, and continuing until _____

_____

_____

_____

_____

_____

_____

_____

_____

_____

_____

_____

_____

_____

_____

_____

_____

_____

_____

_____

_____

_____

_____

_____

Each payment shall be credited first on interest then due and the remainder on principal; and interest shall thereupon cease upon the principal so credited. Should default be made in payment of any installment when due the whole sum of principal and interest shall become immediately due at the option of the holder of this note. Principal and interest payable in lawful money of the United States. If action be instituted on this note I/we promise to pay such sum as the Court may fix as attorney's fees. This note is secured by DEED OF TRUST to
as Trustee.

_____   _____

_____   _____

TO 1930 CA (12-74)

DO NOT DESTROY THIS NOTE

NOTE SECURED BY DEED OF TRUST

give to the beneficiary. This note specifies the amount we borrowed as well as the procedure we've agreed upon for paying it back.

If we don't pay or otherwise fail to meet our obligations, the beneficiary who holds the note notifies the trustee, who then sells our house under the powers we've granted him or her via the trust deed.

It may sound complicated at first, but it's all neat and proper and it does one thing that makes it immensely popular: It avoids court action. We can lose our house under a trust deed without ever having had our day in court!

TRUST DEED CLOCK

Now that we've gotten some basics on how a trust deed operates, let's take a look at the time process we were discussing earlier.

Foreclosure under a trust deed starts when a notice of default is *recorded*. That means when the notice has been duly recorded at the county recorder's office and we've received a copy of it. *Prior to this time we are not in foreclosure*.

We may get threatening letters from the lender. We may get notices that we owe back payments, penalties, and additional interest. But until the notice of default is filed, we are not in foreclosure.

Step One. NOTICE OF DEFAULT FILED

This starts the foreclosure clock ticking. In California (remember each state's laws are somewhat different, so check with an attorney in your state for your procedure) the law prescribes that there is now a three-month waiting period, sometimes also called a redemption period. (Most but not all states have this redemption period.)

Stopping the Foreclosure Clock

In California we can *stop* the foreclosure clock at any time during this three-month period by making up back payments along with any interest and penalties rightfully owed by us.

We can stop the foreclosure clock by negotiating with the lender to either extend, forgive, or delay the money we owe.

We can also *stop* the foreclosure clock, perhaps permanently, by going to court and challenging the trust deed documents.

Finally we can use other means such as bankruptcy (discussed in later chapters) to stop foreclosure.

Let's consider challenging documents in a bit more detail. What we are saying is that *if the lender made a mistake in the documents, a court may throw the whole foreclosure procedure out.* In that case, the lender must start the procedure all over and might not be able to foreclose now or in the future.

That's obviously a very powerful statement. But what kind of mistakes could be in the documents?

There are lots. For example, the document could fail to specify *where* the monthly payment is to be paid. If we don't know where to pay it *as specified in the document,* we may claim that as grounds for not making payments. Historically, this has been used as justification for throwing entire mortgage debts out. (The debt is still owed but might not be collected until the note comes due years and years later.)

The document must also specify the amount of the monthly payment as well as the full amount borrowed.

The document must specify the annual percentage rate ("APR"). This comes under Regulation Z or Truth in Lending, and we'll have a full-chapter discussion of this later.

There are dozens of other items that must specifically and correctly be mentioned in the documents, depending on the state where you live. It is well worth the relatively small expense of having a real estate attorney examine your documents for errors.

Step Two. PUBLISHING

In California after a notice of default has been filed and the three-month redemption period has elapsed, the trustee must now advertise the property for a minimum of twenty-one days.

The advertisement must be published once per week for three weeks and states that the property will be sold at auction at a specified location at a certain date and time at least twenty-one days after publication has been started.

In actual practice the property is sold to the highest bidder or goes back to the beneficiary. (See the chapter on if all else fails for the actual sale procedure and how to bid on your own house.)

The publication is done in a legal, adjudicated newspaper. This is usually a newspaper of relatively small circulation that includes "throwaways" or a legal journal that carries primarily legal notices. (This is why we rarely see such notices in our daily papers.)

Recording Requested by:

AND WHEN RECORDED MAIL TO:

Attn:_____
TS#:_____ _____SPACE ABOVE THIS LINE FOR RECORDER'S USE_____

NOTICE OF TRUSTEE'S SALE

NOTICE

YOU ARE IN DEFAULT UNDER A _____ DATED_____.
UNLESS YOU TAKE ACTION TO PROTECT YOUR PROPERTY, IT MAY BE SOLD AT A PUBLIC SALE. IF
YOU NEED AN EXPLANATION OF THE NATURE OF THE PROCEEDING AGAINST YOU, YOU SHOULD
CONTACT A LAWYER.

ON _____, at _____.M.,
as duly appointed Trustee under and pursuant to Deed of Trust executed by _____
_____ as Trustor for
the benefit and security of _____
_____ as Beneficiary, dated _____
_____, 19   , and recorded as Instrument No. _____
on _____, 19   , _____
County, State of California,

WILL SELL AT PUBLIC AUCTION TO HIGHEST BIDDER FOR CASH, A CASHIER'S CHECK DRAWN ON A
STATE OR NATIONAL BANK, A STATE OR FEDERAL CREDIT UNION, OR A STATE OR FEDERAL SAVINGS
AND LOAN ASSOCIATION DOMICILED IN THE STATE OF CALIFORNIA (payable at time of sale in
lawful money of the United States) at _____
_____
all right title and interest conveyed to and now held by it under said Deed of Trust
in the property situated in said County and State described as:

The street address and other common designation, if any, of the real property described
above is purported to be:

THE UNDERSIGNED TRUSTEE DISCLAIMS ANY LIABILITY FOR INCORRECT INFORMATION FURNISHED.

THAT said sale is made without covenant or warranty regarding title, possession or
encumbrances, or as to insurability of title.

THE total amount of the unpaid balance of said obligations together with advances, and
estimated costs and expenses, is $_____.

THAT notice of breach of said obligation and election to sell said real property was
recorded as Instrument No._____ on_____, 19   , of
Official Records in the office of the County Recorder of _____
County, State of California.

Trustee or party conducting Sale

BY:
Dated:_____   By:_____

NOTICE OF TRUSTEE'S SALE

Stopping the Foreclosure Clock

In California we can *stop* foreclosure any time during these twenty-one days of advertising by four methods:

    1. We can pay off the entire amount of the mortgage plus interest and penalties. (In our earlier example that would be 67,100 dollars.) It's now technically too late to just make up the back payments. We've lost our right to reinstate the mortgage. Now we can only save the property by paying back the full amount we owe.

    2. We can challenge the document as in Step One.

    3. We can negotiate with the lender. In hard times lenders do not want to take back property. If we can demonstrate to the lender that it is to his or her advantage to allow us to continue owning the property and come to an agreement on how to handle the back payments, interest, and penalties owed, the lender *at his or her discretion* can reinstate the trust deed.

    4. We can use other means such as bankruptcy (which will be discussed in later chapters).

Step Three. SALE

As indicated above, after the three-month redemption period and the twenty-one days of advertising, our home is sold to the highest bidder (frequently the beneficiary) on the courthouse steps.

This normally ends the foreclosure clock under a trust deed. This means that we have lost our property for good—but not always.

Under certain circumstances, notably if we file bankruptcy and present our case in a certain way, the courts have in rare instances overturned foreclosure and given the owners back their property!

As we indicated, every state's foreclosure law varies. In Texas you can lose your property in twenty-one days. In Arizona the process takes ninety-one days. In Colorado, even though it is a trust deed state, you can have a period of redemption *even after the sale*, depending on your legal description. You may have seen on the news the farmer in Colorado who lost his farm at a foreclosure auction, where violence broke out in an attempt to stop the sale. He had a "metes and bounds" legal description, and so in Colorado he still has six months to come up with the cash to save his 300-acre farm.

This then is the foreclosure procedure under a trust deed. What's important for us to understand is that we can *stop* foreclosure at almost any point along the way by:

•
•
•

T. S. Officer _____

T. S. No. _____

Your Ref. _____

Gentlemen:

We have recently completed our Trustee's Sale proceedings under your above reference. We are enclosing the Return and Account of Sale, _____

The Trustee's Deed has been forwarded to the office of the county recorder wherein the property was located with instructions to mail it to you after recordation. The processing of the Trustee's Deed by the county recorder normally takes one month.

Please acknowledge receipt of the enclosures and return for our file.

Dated _____

Very truly yours,

Foreclosure Department

TRUSTEE SALE DOCUMENT

TRUSTEE'S SALE GUARANTEE ORDER

NAME
STREET
ADDRESS
CITY &
STATE

Date_____

Liability_____

Attn:_____

REFERENCE NUMBER

Please record **Immediately** the enclosed Notice of Default under the following Deed of Trust where:

_____is duly appointed Trustee under a Deed of Trust

dated   executed by

as Trustor, to secure certain obligations

in favor of

, as beneficiary

recorded   , as instru-   , in   , page   , of Official Records
                          ment no.   book   in the Office of the
Recorder of   County, California, describing land
therein as:

Advise us immediately (within a 24-hour period) of the recording date of the Notice of Default and of any Requests for Notice pursuant to Section 2924b Civil Code.

Thereafter, furnish an original Trustee's Sale Guarantee plus 1-2-3 copies, with a liability as shown above, covering the property described in said Deed of Trust. The Guarantee should include the name of the Judicial Township in which the property is situated and also the name of the newspaper qualified to make publication of our Notice of Sale, together with the days of the week such newspaper is published.

Include with the Guarantee an extra map of the property in question so that it may be used for posting purposes.

Sincerely,

_____

FORM F-2 MPS

TRUSTEE SALE DOCUMENT

T.S. Officer_____

T.S. No._____

Your Ref._____

We are enclosing the Notice of Default and the Declaration of Default in connection with your foreclosure proceeding.

Please check carefully to see that the statement of breach on the enclosed Notice of Default and the Declaration of Default is correctly set forth. Also complete the Declaration of Default with all information called for and then sign, date, and return both documents to us in the enclosed envelope as soon as possible. Also include all receipts for advances already made under the terms of the deed of trust when returning said documents.

Please include your check in the amount shown below under "deposit required" when you return the first above mentioned papers. This amount will cover all fees and expenses until the end of the three month reinstatement period. If there is no reinstatement of your loan, we will ask for the balance of the estimated amount approximately ten days before the end of the three month reinstatement period when we ask for your instructions to proceed with the advertising of the Notice of Trustee's Sale.

Deposit required . . . . $

Balance of estimated total amount required

    before advertising . . . . $

Total estimated amount of fee and expenses

    at the time of sale . . . . $_____

Sincerely,

Foreclosure Department

Enclosures

F-3

TRUSTEE SALE DOCUMENT

T. S. No. _____

Enclosed is a copy of the Notice of Default recorded by us in connection with the above numbered sale proceeding.

The following items are brought to your attention so that the proceeding may be handled as quickly and safely as possible:

1. PROMPTLY FORWARD TO US RECEIPTS COVERING ALL EXPENDITURES MADE BY YOU PURSUANT TO THE TERMS OF THE DEED OF TRUST. This is necessary as we must at all times know the full amount of your claim, AND ONLY THOSE ADVANCES FOR WHICH WE HAVE RECEIPTS MAY BE INCLUDED. Before expending any amounts for work on said property which might be construed as an improvement or a renovation thereof, careful consideration should be given to the fact that said expenditures may not be allowable as advances under the terms of your deed of trust.

2. CAREFUL CONSIDERATION SHOULD BE GIVEN TO THE POSSIBILITY THAT THE DEFAULT MAY BE CURED IF AN AMOUNT IS TENDERED WHICH IS LESS THAN THE TOTAL AMOUNT NECESSARY TO REINSTATE. Such a partial acceptance might invalidate the proceedings thus far accomplished. The amounts necessary to reinstate generally include the delinquent amounts on the note, advances made pursuant to the terms of the deed of trust (if any), interest on the advances made, and the Trustee's fee and expenses.

3. SECTION 2924C OF THE CALIFORNIA CIVIL CODE PROVIDES THAT THE BENEFICIARY UNDER THE DEED OF TRUST MUST ACCEPT MONEY FOR REINSTATEMENT IF THE PROPER AMOUNTS ARE TENDERED TO THE BENEFICIARY DURING THE THREE-MONTH PERIOD FROM THE RECORDING DATE OF THE NOTICE OF DEFAULT. If the amount tendered covers all items mentioned in the above paragraph, you should notify us immediately. We will then send you for your signature a rescission of the Notice of Default. When you return the signed rescission we will have it recorded and the deed of trust will then be reinstated.

Thank you for your cooperation.

Yours very truly,

Foreclosure Department

Enclosure

F-4

TRUSTEE SALE DOCUMENT

DECLARATION OF DEFAULT CONTINUED

that by reason thereof, the undersigned hereby declares all sums secured by said Deed of Trust immediately due and payable; that there is now due, owing and unpaid said note(s) the remaining principal sum of $_____ with interest thereon

from _____

as in said note(s) provided and all sums properly advanced or expended under the terms of said Deed of Trust, with the interest therein provided. Therefore you are hereby requested and directed to sell the property now covered thereby to satisfy the obligations so secured. Said Deed of Trust, note(s) and receipts for sums advanced are hereby handed you, and you are instructed to record the accompanying Notice of Default. The undersigned will deliver to you receipts for all sums, if any, hereafter properly advanced or expended under the terms of said Deed of Trust. Immediately upon payment thereof. If, prior to sale, immediately upon payment in full be made to you of all sums herein declared to be due, as well as any advances hereafter properly made, or which you have been advised, together with your fees and expenses, you shall cancel said note or notes and reconvey said property, as provided in said Deed of Trust, but without expense to the undersigned. The undersigned hereby guarantees payment of all fees and expenses of said Trusts and of the Trustee pertaining to said sale.

Dated,_____

THE PROPERTY ADDRESS IS:

_____
Number and Street

_____
City, State and Zip Code

IT IS THE OBLIGATION OF THE BENEFICIARY TO FURNISH ALL ADDRESSES KNOWN FOR THE TRUSTOR, GIVE NAMES AND ADDRESSES OF ALL PARTIES HAVING AN INTEREST (JUNIOR DEED OF TRUST HOLDERS, OTHER LIEN HOLDERS, LESSEES, ETC.) IN THE PROPERTY.

Names	Street and Number or Mailing Address	City, Town or Post Office	Nature of Claim or Interest

---

DECLARATION OF DEFAULT

TO: _____

Trust dated _____

_____ YOU ARE HEREBY NOTIFIED: That you are duly appointed Trustee under a Deed of

executed by _____

as Trustor, to secure certain obligations

in favor of _____ as beneficiary

recorded _____, in book _____, page _____ of Official Records in the Office of the

Recorder of _____ County, California, describing land therein as:

_____ as Instru- ment no. _____

including _____ note for the sum of $_____ said obligations

that a breach of, and default in, the obligations for which such Deed of Trust is security has occurred in that payment has not been made of:

CONTINUED ON REVERSE SIDE

FORM F-3 MPS

TRUSTEE'S SALE DOCUMENT

RECORDING REQUESTED BY

AND WHEN RECORDED MAIL TO:

Name ⌈
Street
Address
City
State ⌊
Zip

MAIL TAX STATEMENTS TO:

——SPACE ABOVE THIS LINE FOR RECORDER'S USE——

Name ⌈
Street
Address
City
State ⌊
Zip

Trustee's Deed Upon Sale

Trustee Sale No._____

The undersigned grantor declares:
    (1) The Grantee herein was—was not the foreclosing beneficiary.
    (2) The amount of the unpaid dept together with costs was...$_____
    (3) The amount paid by the grantee at the trustee sale was..$_____
    (4) The documentary transfer tax is...$_____
    (5) The survey monument fee is..$_____
    (6) Said property is in ( ) unincorporated area: ( ) City of _____, and
                                               (herein called Trustee), as the
duly appointed Trustee under the Deed of Trust hereinafter described, does hereby grant and convey, but without warranty, express or
implied, to

(herein called Grantee), all of its right, title and interest in and to that certain property situated in the City of
, County of , State of California, described as follows:

TRUSTEE STATES THAT:

This conveyance is made pursuant to the powers conferred upon Trust by that certain Deed of Trust dated
and executed by
as trustor, and recorded
in Book , Instrument No. , Page , of Official Records of
County, California, and after fulfillment of the conditions specified in said Deed of Trust authorizing this conveyance.
Default occurred as set forth in a Notice of Default and Election to Sell which was recorded in the office of the Recorder of said County.
All requirements of law regarding the mailing and recording of copies of notices and the posting and publication and recording of
copies of the Notice of Sale have been complied with.
Said property as sold by said Trustee at public auction on at the place named in the Notice of Sale,
in the County of , California, in which the property is situated. Grantee being the highest bidder at such sale, became the purchaser of
said property and paid therefor to said Trustee the amount bid, being $, in lawful money of the United States,
or by the satisfaction, pro tanto, of the obligations then secured by said Deed of Trust.
IN WITNESS WHEREOF, said , as Trustee, has
this day, caused its corporate name and seal to be hereunto affixed by its Vice-President and Assistant Secretary, thereunto duly
authorized by resolution of its Board of Directors.

                                   as Trustee aforesaid.

Dated: _____

    STATE OF CALIFORNIA
    COUNTY OF   } SS.   By _____

On this_____ day of_____, 19_____,
before me, the undersigned, a Notary Public in and for said County and State,
personally appeared _____   By _____
known to me to be the_____President,
and _____
known to me to be the_____Secretary
of the corporation that executed the within instrument, and known to me to be the
persons who executed the within instrument on behalf of the corporation therein
named and, acknowledged to me that such corporation executed the same,
purusant to its laws, or a resolution of its Board of Directors.
WITNESS my hand and official seal.

Signature_____

_____
       Name (Typed or Printed)   (This area for official seal)

TRUSTEE'S DEED

1. making up back payments (first three months)
2. challenging the documents
3. negotiating with the lender
4. paying off the debt (as, for example, by refinancing)

We'll discuss these options in much greater detail in later chapters, but now let's turn to the other major document used on home loans, the mortgage.

MORTGAGE FORECLOSURE

While most states now use the trust deed, many still rely on the mortgage. The mortgage differs from the trust deed in several ways. One important way is that a mortgage can only be foreclosed through court action (as opposed to the trust deed, which can be foreclosed by means of a trustee's sale handled outside of court).

Another difference is that instead of three parties to the document, there are only two:

Mortgagor (borrower)

Mortgagee (lender)

In addition there is a single document that spells out the property that serves as the collateral for the loan, the amount borrowed, the interest rate, the monthly payments, and the other terms and conditions.

The mortgage, however, has similarities to the trust deed. There is a clock that runs from the time formal notice of foreclosure is given. There are specified steps that must be taken. There is usually a period of redemption. As with the trust deed, foreclosure may be stopped at almost any point in the process by:

1. making up back payments with interest and penalties
2. challenging the documents
3. negotiating with the lender
4. using other means, which will be discussed in later chapters.

Let's take it one step at a time:

Step One. ACCELERATION

The first step in foreclosure under a mortgage is usually acceleration of the debt. We have already seen a typical letter of acceleration. It notifies us (the mortgagor) that we are in default and that the lender is accelerating the mortgage or calling it in. Here is the typical clause in a mortgage that allows the lender to accelerate:

At the option of the mortgagee, the entire principal sum along with interest shall become due: if the mortgagor is more than fifteen days late in making any payment of principal or interest; if the mortgagor fails to timely make any tax or assessment payment; if the mortgagor fails to maintain adequate fire insurance; [etc.].

The lender has an option here. He or she could choose to accelerate only a portion of the mortgage, say just the back payments due plus interest and penalties. If he or she does this, however, and we make a partial payment (which is accepted), and then we don't make additional payments, the lender has to start the whole procedure from scratch, which is costly and time-consuming. Therefore, most lenders, to give themselves the maximum advantage, ask for full payment right at the beginning.

How to Stop Foreclosure
The lender, particularly during harsh economic times, is not looking to take back the property. He or she is looking to negotiate. Once we receive a letter of acceleration, we can normally reinstate the loan (at the lender's option) by making up back payments and penalties. We can reinstate, normally, right up until the time the house is sold and in some cases even afterward! (We can do this by refinancing, by selling, by taking in partners, or by dozens of other alternatives.)

We can negotiate with the lender. We can explain that we are out of work or are ill. If the lender will grant us forbearance, we say we will make up the money eventually. Forbearance simply means holding off foreclosure. We might agree to make smaller payments or no payments for six months, adding the unpaid amounts to the loan balance or some other similar arrangement.

We can also challenge the documents in the same manner as we challenged the trust deed documents.

We can resort to other methods, such as checking to see if this is a usurious loan, or a Regulation Z violation, (discussed later).

Many lenders will file a notice of acceleration at the drop of a hat. It is easy and inexpensive to do. For them to proceed further, however, costs real money. To proceed further means they will have to use an attorney and their costs could be anywhere from 1,000 to 5,000 dollars. That's a lot of money to lay out in cash with only a dubious hope of recovering it later. Most lenders would rather negotiate with the borrower. That's an important point I keep emphasizing and which we should always remember.

Step Two. COMPLAINT FOR NONPAYMENT

This will be filed by the mortgagee's attorney. A summons is then sent to the mortgagor.

The time period here is flexible, usually depending on the availability of courtroom space. It could be as short as a few weeks, as long as six months, or longer.

The mortgagor (borrower) must answer the complaint one way or another.

How to Stop Foreclosure

As before, we can stop the process by making up the back-owed monies, by negotiating with the lender, or by other actions, one of which we'll discuss now.

Typically a mortgagor will answer the complaint by indicating that he or she is indeed in default and behind in payments. After all, that is the case.

If the mortgagor does this, then the procedure moves ahead rapidly. The mortgagee files a motion for a summary judgment. A referee is appointed, a judgment sale time approved, and the property is sold to satisfy the mortgage debt.

On the other hand, the mortgagor can secure the services of an attorney and deny the complaint. If this happens, then usually a trial date is set.

Depending on how tight the court calendar is, this trial date may be anywhere from a few weeks to half a year or longer away. During this time period, the mortgagor can remain in the property and probably does not have to make additional payments. This can be a highly effective *delaying* tactic.

At the trial the mortgagor can challenge the mortgage documents and if successful, potentially have the foreclosure thrown out. The mortgagor's attorney can also present extenuating circumstances such as threats the lender may have made to the mortgagor or improper procedure followed in the foreclosure process. This could result in the foreclosure complaint being denied and the mortgagee having to start all over again with the letter of acceleration. Here the mortgagor's goal might be to delay the final sale of the property.

Step Three. THE COURT FINDS
IN FAVOR OF THE MORTGAGEE
If the mortgagor loses the trial, then the judge usually appoints a referee to inventory and evaluate the property. The referee can take from a few weeks to many months to accomplish his or her duties.

Appeal the Foreclosure Verdict
While the referee is working, the mortgagor can launch an appeal of the trial. This may or may not stop the referee's work, but it will usually postpone the eventual sale until the appeal is heard. Appeals notoriously take a long time. If, however, the mortgagee can demonstrate that the appeal is groundless, it might be denied out of hand as a delaying tactic.

The mortgagor can negotiate with the lender.

The mortgagor can also file bankruptcy or start other proceedings to halt the foreclosure.

Step Four. FORECLOSURE JUDGMENT
The referee reports back to the court, and the judge issues a foreclosure judgment. The property is advertised (the time period for advertising varies enormously from state to state) and the property is sold on the courthouse steps to the highest bidder (usually the mortgagee).

Step Five. REDEMPTION PERIOD
Unlike most trust deeds, a mortgage almost always carries with it an equity of redemption.

The origin of this goes back to English common law. In the past the rights of the lender far superseded any rights of the borrower. If Sally borrowed 1,000 dollars from John, put up her property as collateral, and then failed to repay as agreed, John had the right to claim Sally's property. He, in effect, could foreclose.

This, however, worked some injustice. Perhaps Sally wanted to repay but couldn't at the time. There had been bad weather, which ruined or delayed her crops. She had been ill. Her money had been stolen. She lost her property because of events beyond her control.

The law recognized the importance of a person's property above the value of money, so the concept of redemption came into existence about the middle of the 1800s. Yes, John could take Sally's property back when she failed to pay. But if Sally repaid within a reasonable time after he had taken it, he had to give it back. By repaying, Sally could *redeem* her property even after it had been lost.

This equity or interest in redemption persists today in most mortgage states. It usually does not occur where a trust deed is used because foreclosure occurs outside of court. (In trust deed states a note for a trust deed can be foreclosed through a judicial foreclosure and not by the trustee and if that is done, redemption may exist.)

How to Stop Foreclosure
It is technically inaccurate to say that we can stop foreclosure once a sale has occurred. If we have an equity of redemption, however, we may be able to get our property back. If we lose our property in a foreclosure sale, our equity of redemption clock starts when the sale is concluded. It runs for as long as is allowed in our state. (The actual period may be from a few weeks to several years.)

During this time period we can redeem our property by repaying the amount of the mortgage plus court costs, interest, and penalties.

During the equity of redemption period you are usually permitted to live in your home. If the property were sold for far less than its true value, the equity of redemption can be a highly useful tool. If, for example, your property was sold for 67,100 dollars but today its true value is 100,000 dollars, you might very seriously consider selling to a third party and exercising your equity of redemption. By doing so you would instantly gain a profit of the difference between the sales price and the current value. (Your profit here would be 32,900 dollars.)

These then are the basic steps involved in foreclosure on a mortgage.

I would be remiss, however, if I didn't point out that there are other methods of foreclosure in some states.

STRICT FORECLOSURE

Used principally in Vermont and Connecticut, strict foreclosure does not involve a sale of property. A court hearing is held to determine if the mortgagee does indeed have the right to foreclose. If such a right is determined, the court then awards the property to the mortgagee.

Stopping Strict Foreclosure

This involves the same methods as in the case of the trust deed or the mortgage. Because it can move faster, however, it is important to be timely in our moves.

The big disadvantage with strict foreclosure for the borrower is that because there is no sale, there can never be any leftovers. For example, let's consider judicial foreclosure (which we discussed earlier). Let's say we owe 5,000 dollars on a 50,000-dollar home. Under a sale, the property would go to the highest bidder. Let's say the highest bidder offered 40,000 dollars.

The first 5,000 dollars would go to the mortgagee. We, the borrower, would get the balance of 35,000 dollars.

Under strict foreclosure, however, the property would simply be turned over to the mortgagee (lender). We would not get the entire 40,000 dollars—we would get nothing. The mortgagee would get the entire benefit. For this reason it is very important to reach an amicable conclusion with the lender before court disposition in a state involving strict foreclosure.

ENTRY FORECLOSURE

This is still used by a few New England states. Under entry foreclosure, the mortgagee forecloses by *peacefully* throwing out the mortgagor. The mortgagee then takes possession and after holding the property for a specified time acquires title.

The procedure varies from state to state but can be very swift. As in strict foreclosure, every effort should be made to negotiate with the lender *before* this takes place. (Entry foreclosure is essentially the same as strict foreclosure without the benefits of court action since here again the mortgagor gets nothing.)

DEFICIENCY JUDGMENTS

In a judicial foreclosure (such as discussed under a mortgage) if the property does not bring enough money at a sale, the court may award a judgment for the deficiency to the mortgagee on the mortgagor's other personal or real property. In other words, if our property doesn't bring enough to satisfy the mortgage, we could be liable for the difference!

In Oregon and Washington deficiency judgments are not allowed on purchase money mortgages or mortgages that were used as part of the purchase price of a home. (This is opposed to, for example, a mortgage that was taken out after the home was purchased to allow a home improvement.) Two other states do not allow deficiency judgments—South Dakota and Nebraska.

PROCEDURAL RULES FOR STOPPING FORECLOSURE

We've very briefly covered the foreclosure procedure and some of the documents used in it. It's important to remember not just the procedure, but also what we must do to *stop* foreclosure.

Here are rules for stopping foreclosure:

1. Learn the clock. Know the important dates. *Act timely.*

2. Reinstate the loan *before* the clock runs out. *Refinance, sell, take in a partner, and be creative in raising the money to reinstate.* (Solutions will be discussed in later chapters.)

3. Study the procedure *for your state.* Libraries have books giving this information. If you can't find it, an attorney can usually tell you this information in a few minutes. *Learn the rights your state gives you to stop foreclosure.*

4. Study your loan documents. Are there any typos? Take them to an attorney. *Challenge documents* where appropriate.

5. Talk to your lender. Remember, your lender doesn't want foreclosure either. Give the lender half a reason not to foreclose and he or she will probably jump at it. *Communicate, communicate, communicate—honestly!*

6. Consider desperate measures such as fighting foreclosure in court and filing bankruptcy (others will be discussed in later chapters.)

In nearly all cases foreclosure can be avoided or postponed, providing we act timely.

If there are any two pieces of advice I would give a person who is facing foreclosure right now, they would have to be:

PAY ATTENTION TO THE CLOCK

Foreclosure is a procedure and there are definite time limits involved. If you don't act timely and you lose your rights, don't go complaining. You are responsible for learning the time constraints for your state. If you don't, you may lose by default.

COMMUNICATE, COMMUNICATE, COMMUNICATE

Once again, remember that the lender doesn't want your property. Lenders want the money. If they get your property in a depressed market, they won't get the money. The lender usually wants to help you get out of foreclosure as much as you want to get out. Give your lender half a chance to help and he or she may bail you out.

Now, assuming that we understand the foreclosure procedure and the rudiments of how to stop it, let's take a look at our house and see if it is really worth saving!

Chapter Two
IS YOUR PROPERTY WORTH SAVING?

"Cadillac Fairview defaulted on an $84 million mortgage on a Manhattan office site that it bought last year for $105 million, and the site is being taken back by its former owner, Citibank. The Canadian developer walked away from a $21 million down payment on the property."
—*The Wall Street Journal*

Just because your property is going into foreclosure doesn't necessarily mean that it is worth saving. Your equity in the property may be so small that you would be better off letting the property go.

That may seem like a difficult statement to live with, particularly in a book such as this, which is dedicated to stopping foreclosure. But there comes a time, and in foreclosure it comes early on, when we have to come up with a winning strategy. Depending on our equity in our house, that winning strategy may mean letting the property go.

HOW MUCH EQUITY DO YOU REALLY HAVE?

Many people today have less equity than they think in their property. The reason is that prices have been going down for homes in most areas. (When prices go up, people tend to think that they have less equity than they really have.)

Let's look at it this way. If you bought your home any time since 1980 and you put twenty percent or less down, you may not have enough equity today in your property to make it worth saving.

The biggest reason is a loss in value. In most areas the decline in prices has been between five and ten percent of the full house value. If you put down twenty percent and the house has declined in value by ten percent, your equity has been cut in half. You only have a ten percent equity.

Sometimes this is a difficult point to understand, so let's look at an example. Let's say we bought a house in 1980 for 100,000 dollars and put twenty percent or 20,000 dollars down.

$100,000	(value at purchase)
−20,000	(down payment)
$80,000	(mortgage [or mortgages])

Now it's today and the price of the house has declined by ten percent:

$100,000	(original value)
×90%	(rate of current value)
$90,000	(current value)
−80,000	(less mortgage)
$10,000	(current equity)

Our equity has been eaten up by the decline in value of the property.

You may argue, "My house hasn't declined in value."

I hope you are right. But with the recession, high interest rates, and governmental rulings in many cases preventing assumption of existing low interest rate mortgages, housing prices in most areas have indeed fallen.

Of course, not all of the decline has been visible. In some cases it has been in the form of the seller taking less cash down and carrying the balance in the form of a low interest rate "second." (But even that practice will greatly decline now that many existing first mortgages are no longer assumable.)

Okay, let's say that maybe your equity has dropped so that instead of twenty percent, it's only fifteen or even ten percent. Isn't that worth saving?

Maybe not: Consider, the only time that we can really be justified in saying what our equity is is when we sell. Until that time our equity is just an idea in our heads. It's when we sell that this idea turns into cash.

But selling real estate is costly. There is a commission to pay (often anywhere from five to seven percent). There are closing costs, including title insurance, escrow fees, document fees, and the cost of getting the house in shape to meet termite, FHA (Federal Housing Authority), GI (Government Inspection), or other required clearances. These costs can often eat up most of the remainder of our equity. Consider the enclosed worksheet for a property sold through a broker with FHA or GI financing:

123 DAMASCUS AVE.

Loan Information

First mortgage	$70,000
Second mortgage	10,000
Back payments on "first"	2,500
Back payments on "second"	500
Other costs to clear foreclosure	1,000
Total loan payoffs	$84,000

COST OF SELLING TO THE SELLER
($100,000 sales price)

Commission	$6,000
Four points for new FHA or GI loan	4,000
Title insurance policy	300
Escrow fee	500
Home warranty policy	300
Document fees	100
Transfer tax	500
Termite work	500
Other repairs	2,500
Three months payments while in escrow	2,400
Tax proration	800
Total sales costs	$17,900

NET RETURN TO SELLER UPON SALE

From sale	$100,000
Less sales costs	−17,900
Less loan payoffs	−84,000
Loss on sale	($1,900)

That's right. It could cost roughly 2,000 dollars out of pocket, not to mention the lost equity, for the seller to dump his or her house.

Of course this example has been exaggerated to make a point. But it hasn't been exaggerated that much. With declining values and with the costs of selling being so high, many of us find ourselves in just the situation described.

DO YOU HAVE A SALVAGEABLE EQUITY?

To find out, I suggest you take the time to fill out the following forms. They will tell you where you stand. The first sheet will help you to determine what you actually owe on your present loan. The second sheet will help to determine what the costs of a sale would be if made today. They will show you what the true equity of your home is.

Now you should have a pretty good idea of what the equity in your home really is. Your next question is, "Is my equity large enough to be worth saving?

One rule of thumb is that if your equity *before* costs of sale and loan payoffs isn't at least ten to fifteen percent of the value, you probably don't have enough to fight over from a financial viewpoint. But the emotional side of losing a property you love is such that it can pay to fight for a property even if there is no equity.

If you don't have enough real equity in your home, stop making your payments now!

If you don't have enough equity in your home to justify an all-out attempt to stop foreclosure, don't make another payment. You are just throwing your money down the drain.

Take the money you would otherwise be paying to your mortgage, taxes, and insurance and put it into a high-yielding money market account. Each month instead of giving that money for the house, you'll be saving it. After a year, you may have enough to make a down payment on another house or get started financially elsewhere.

EXISTING LOAN INFORMATION AND FORECLOSURE WORKSHEET

FIRST MORTGAGE DELINQUENCY
        Date of Default.....................................
        Beneficiary...
        Phone number..
        Loan Type...
        Percentage Rate.....................................
        Balance due $..........
        Monthly pmt $..........
        Date of last payment...........
        Date payments due..............
        Costs (including attorney fees)....................

        Total due to reinstate mortgage (principal, interest, fees
                and charges) $......................

SECOND MORTGAGE DELINQUENCY
        Date of Default.....................................
        Beneficiary...
        Phone number..
        Loan Type...
        Percentage Rate.....................................
        Balance due $..........
        Monthly pmt $..........
        Date of last payment...........
        Date payments due..............
        Costs (including attorney fees)....................

        Total due to reinstate mortgage (principal, interest, fees
                and charges) $......................

THIRD MORTGAGE DELINQUENCY
        Date of Default.....................................
        Beneficiary...
        Phone number..
        Loan Type...
        Percentage Rate.....................................
        Balance due $..........
        Monthly pmt $..........
        Date of last payment...........
        Date payments due..............
        Costs (including attorney fees)....................

        Total due to reinstate mortgage (principal, interest, fees
                and charges) $......................

EXISTING LOAN INFORMATION AND
FORECLOSURE WORKSHEET

To put it another way, don't beat a dead horse. If you're going to lose anyway, you might as well get out as much as you can.

Of course, this raises another question for most people: "If I don't make the payment, where will I live?"

The answer is that you'll live in your house until foreclosure is final. You'll take steps to see that the finalization doesn't come for many, many months. (In some cases it can be pushed back by years!)

Here are some of the steps you can take to delay the foreclosure sale of your house:

1. Offer the lender a deed to the property in lieu of foreclosure *if* you agree not to fight foreclosure and *if* the lender agrees to allow you to stay in the property without making payments for a set period of time (try for a year).

As we've seen, the foreclosure process can be lengthy and costly. Here you are offering the lender a way to determine the exact date foreclosure will take place and a way to eliminate all the foreclosure costs. In today's market a lender may figure, "If I don't agree, it will still take me at least a year to get them out. This way they get out and I save a year's worth of legal costs and hassle."

Besides giving you a place to live rent free for a year, there is another advantage to this technique—it preserves your credit. If you give a deed in lieu of foreclosure, no foreclosure takes place. Your credit rating never need show the difficulties you were in.

If you give a deed in lieu of foreclosure, be sure you have a *written* agreement with the lender specifying that you are allowed to remain in the property rent free for the agreed-upon term. You might want to have an attorney draw this up for you.

2. Ask for forbearance. Here you are asking the lender to stop foreclosure and instead help you through some difficult times. You are asking the lender to reduce or suspend your monthly payments for a while (ask for at least twelve months to start).

Most lenders take back property only as a last resort. If they take it back they have to support it—that is, they have to see that it is maintained, and they have to make a costly effort to sell it.

Under forbearance, they don't take it back; rather you, the

borrower, maintain it. They don't lose the monthly payments, at least as far as their books are concerned. The monthly payments you don't make are usually added to the principal of the loan. You end up still owing the money, only now you pay it back over twenty or thirty years.

If forbearance is given, you have a decision to make. You can either continue on with your strategy of dumping the property, or (what probably makes better sense now) you can now see your way clear to live there for the time of the forbearance and then at the end of the time, decide whether it makes sense to wage an all-out effort to save the house or let it go.

3. You can take other action such as challenging documents or filing bankruptcy. Your goal here is not to stop foreclosure but to delay it. You want to live in your house rent free for as long as possible while your nest egg is building in a money market account.

IF YOU HAVE A LARGE EQUITY

On the other hand, you may find that you have a substantial equity in your property. You've carefully gone over the worksheets and you discover that, yes indeed, there's something there worth fighting for.

If that's the case, then you should be prepared to fight tooth and nail to save your property. In the remaining chapters we'll go into great detail on the various means that can be taken to stop foreclosure and save a house that has equity.

Chapter Three
NEGOTIATING WITH A BANK OR SAVINGS AND LOAN

"The first and greatest commandment is, 'Don't let them scare you!'"
—Elmer Davis

To begin, let's consider what I feel should be the very first step in *stopping* foreclosure: going to see the lender and beginning the process of negotiation. Negotiation begins with an understanding of whom we are dealing with. We don't negotiate with a marble building that has the words XYZ Savings and Loan in twelve-foot letters at the top—we negotiate with people. If we understand their pressures and their goals, then we will be in a position to show them that it is to their advantage to do what we want.

WHO IS YOUR LENDER?

There are basically two kinds of lenders, and each kind has a different viewpoint. A bank or a savings and loan is an institutional lender. This means that the institution lends the money. The person we deal with isn't lending his or her own money—he or she is lending the institution's money.

The other kind is a private lender. A private lender is indeed a person loaning his or her money. A private lender has a much different viewpoint from that of an institutional lender. We'll deal with negotiating with private lenders in the next chapter.

The goals of an institutional lender are usually twofold:

1. The lender doesn't want to show a loss.
2. The lender wants a steady cash flow.

A loss would come about if the lender had to foreclose and then had to resell for *less than the total of the money loaned plus interest and charges*. Notice that a loss does not come about simply by foreclosing. When a lender forecloses, it is simply a bookkeeping entry. Instead of a mortgage owned, the books now show a house owned. In both cases this is an asset. It is only when the house is ultimately disposed of for a loss that the loss shows up on the books.

A steady cash flow comes from borrowers regularly making their monthly payments. If the lender can count on the borrower making a payment each month, cash is flowing in. This cash is used to offset the lender's other expenses.

When the cash flow is interrupted, the lender is not getting the money needed to pay expenses. Usually lenders maintain a delicate balance between cash flow and expenses. Typically they have very little margin to play with.

HOW TO TALK TO AN INSTITUTIONAL LENDER

Once we know we're dealing with an institution whose goal is to avoid loss and maintain cash flow, we must come to terms with the motivations of the individual representing the institution.

Understanding the individual representing the lender is very easy if we understand why officers of banks and savings and loans usually get fired. There are three reasons:

1. making bad loans
2. making bad loans
3. making bad loans

If we're dealing with the person who originally made the loan to us, we're in great shape. This person has his or her hide to protect. If we are dealing with a different officer, which is more likely, this officer is going to want to be sure that whatever he or she does doesn't turn a bad situation into a worse one. This person doesn't want a senior officer later to say, "You messed up on that mortgage. You cost the bank money."

How does this officer cost the bank money?

If he or she forecloses, there is an interruption of cash flow—a no-no. If he or she forecloses and goes to sale, taking the property back, there are costs—lots of them (like legal fees, escrow service charges, title search expenses, and so on). If the property taken back can't be sold to cover the mortgage and all these costs, there is a loss to the lender—another no-no.

All of which is to say that the officer who represents the institutional lender should be highly motivated to come to some sort of a solution other than foreclosure. This officer may find foreclosure as distasteful as we do.

Once we understand this, we can talk to this lender from a position of mutual interest. Both of us are interested in finding a solution to the problem.

This is a subtle but important point. Too often borrowers facing foreclosure go to lenders and try to sweet-talk them into helping. The borrower's attitude is, "I'm in trouble and you have a lot of money—it is your duty to help me." That doesn't work. It is like getting a ticket. A good attitude goes a long way in determining the officer's decision to give you a warning or a ticket.

Lenders simply don't respond well to the poor me appeal. A person in foreclosure might indeed have a very sad tale to tell. But playing on the lender's sympathy will only get you so far. You might even go to the same church as the lender. Maybe you were boyhood chums. It means *nothing*! That is not as important as your attitude. No lender is going to put his or her job on the line to help you if you do not explain your current problem realistically and why things are going to get better.

On the other hand, a more helpful attitude is to point out that it is not just I who is in trouble with this foreclosure. It is the both of *us*. Finding a solution will help the lender and his or her institution as much or even more than it will help you. Take this attitude and you'll have the lender's attention.

PROCEDURE FOR NEGOTIATING
WITH AN INSTITUTIONAL LENDER

First call and ask to talk directly to the person who is in charge of your mortgage. It may be someone in the collection department, or it might be the officer who originally placed the loan. Maybe it's an officer at the downtown branch. Find out who it is, no matter how many people you have to go through. It won't do any good to talk with someone's secretary. You have to find the person in charge and deal directly with that person. He or she is the only person in a position to make concessions.

Second, once you've identified the person, say something such as, "I need advice on *our* mortgage. Could I take you out to lunch Tuesday or come in on Thursday afternoon?"

Bank officers and savings and loan officers are not usually well paid. Not too many people offer to take them out to lunch. If you make it clear you're not going to cry on their shoulders, but rather you want to talk earnestly with them, there's a good chance they will take you up on your offer. It's a lot easier discussing the problem over lunch.

If lunch isn't a possibility, secure an appointment in the person's office for as soon as possible.

Third, after you've secured an appointment, write a letter or note to the person. Tell him or her something such as:

> Dear —,
> I want to thank you for taking the time to share your expertise with me. I am looking forward to our lunch this Friday at 12:00.
> Thanks again for your help.

Fourth, on the day of the appointment, call the lender's secretary and say something such as, "This is —. I am calling to confirm my appointment with Mr. (Mrs., Ms.) —. Thank you."

The purpose of the calls and the letter is to establish that you operate in a professional manner and are aware of the gravity of the situation. At the same time you are showing that you are not panicky. Finally, you are demonstrating an eagerness to come up with a solution.

Fifth, when you meet with the lender, go through the following procedure:

1. Thank him or her for seeing you.

2. State that you need advice regarding your mortgage.

3. Explain that you have a *temporary* problem and that you want to communicate closely. Explain that you are sure the lender can show you some options and give you some ideas about overcoming the problem. Say that you are seeking his or her help in solving the problem.

4. Discuss the problem openly. A good attitude is to give the impression that, "I would like to brainstorm with you some of my options." Ask the lender to tell you what he or she sees as your options.

5. As the lender gives you options, write each down. He or she may have some pearls there that you won't want to lose. You will also impress the lender with your businesslike manner. The lender might feel that you are the sort of person who can really turn this thing around, and the lender might mention a few options that he or she normally wouldn't give to the person who comes in whining and seeking pity. Pay close attention to the options. The degree to which the lender is flexible will tell you just how anxious he or she is to avoid foreclosure. After the lender has exhausted the options, review them with him or her. You can say something such as, "I am hearing three options: 1. —, 2. —, 3. —. Is that correct?"

6. Ask a lot of well-thought-out questions. The problem here is that it is very difficult for most of us to come up with well-thought-out questions on the spur of the moment. The solution is to have them well in advance. Have them ready before you go in. Then as the lender responds, write down the answers.

Here are some sample questions:

"Could you explain the foreclosure process?"

"What do lenders do with properties they take back through foreclosure?"

"Are lenders anxious to get properties back in today's market?"

"Can you help me get a replacement loan?"

"Working out a solution would be preferable to *your* getting the property back, wouldn't it?"

"Today's economy is causing people who normally are solid citizens to have trouble making payments, isn't it?"

"The Feds are creating a liquidity crisis for everyone, aren't they?"

The last three questions are designed to get a yes answer. Any lender is going to have a lot of trouble answering no to any of them. Once the lender is in the frame of mind for answering yes, yes, yes, he or she is more inclined to react positively to specific options and solutions to your problem.

7. Make an emotional appeal. *Show* the lender how important the house, your credit, and his or her well-being are to you. Get the lender emotionally involved with you in saving your property. Talk about your son's Little League team and your daughter's school choir. Tell specific stories of the pain it will cause your family (not you) if you lose your property.

At this point, we hope, you've come up with some solutions. Perhaps there's forbearance. Maybe a refinance is in order. A different kind of loan may prove helpful. We'll discuss all these options and many more in later chapters. But now let's assume that these seven steps didn't lead to the conclusion you wanted. Let's say that this lender is acting tough. This lender won't help. He or she will barely communicate.

HOW DO YOU NEGOTIATE WITH AN UNWILLING LENDER?

If you're getting nowhere with the good guy approach, it's probably time to bring out the bad guy. (If the lender gets put out by the bad guy, you can always revert to the good guy.)

Put away the notepad you've been writing on. Pull out a tape recorder and say, "You don't mind if I tape this, do you? I find that I can't always take notes fast enough, and you wouldn't want me to miss any important points, would you?"

Turn on the machine and put the microphone on the lender's desk.

This is extremely intimidating. The lender is suddenly seeing a new side to you. He or she doesn't know what you're going to do with that tape. Are you contemplating some sort of court action? Will that tape be used in court? Will it be played back to the lender's superiors?

Usually the lender will have a moment of concern, and then proceed. Why should he or she worry? The lender has you over a barrel, not the other way around. The lender is the one threatening foreclosure.

Now you begin a different set of questions:

1. "Could you explain Regulation Z to me?"

The lender may jump out of the seat at this. Regulation Z is the Truth in Lending regulation and an increasing number of foreclosures are being thrown out because the lender made some technical mistake in filling out the forms and trying to adhere to the rules of Regulation Z. (We'll cover Regulation Z in a separate chapter.)

If you're talking Regulation Z, could it be because someone has told you that you might get the foreclosure thrown out on a technicality? You've got the lender worried.

2. "Can I please have a copy of the Regulation Z documents?"

Why would you want a copy of the documents unless you want to see if the lender complied with Regulation Z? How can the lender refuse to give you copies? If he or she does, will that influence a court decision on the foreclosure later on? If you get the copies, what are the chances you could find an error? (The chances are better than you think, given the complexity of the regulation.)

3. "What would be the impact if I file for bankruptcy the day before the foreclosure sale?"

The impact almost certainly would be an immediate and automatic stay of the foreclosure. The property could be tied up for months, maybe years. During that time you certainly wouldn't make any payments. The bank would lose interest, attorney's fees, and what could be most costly, time. I guarantee the lender knows this possibility. What's important is that suddenly the lender knows you know it, too.

4. "Is it true that I can switch from one chapter of the bankruptcy law to another? Is it true that after I get through filing, even if the foreclosure ultimately gets thrown out of court, my wife [husband] can file and start the whole thing over again?"

"Oh my gosh," the lender must be thinking. "You're a real stinker. You could tie this property up for years—and I'll be the one who recommended we proceed with foreclosure. This one will go down on my record."

Usually by about this time the lender has a sudden change of heart. Perhaps you might want to go over those options available to you with him or her one more time. Maybe there are one or two options in there the lender didn't mention that might help you out.

Now it's time to put away the bad guy and bring out the good guy again. As the lender gets more cordial, the tape recorder goes away. "Maybe I won't need this," you explain. The notepad comes out and you begin to work together to come up with a solution.

If you've already got a plan in mind, now's the time to pop it to the lender. You can be sure the lender will take it seriously. Maybe you want forbearance. Maybe you want a graduated payment mortgage (with lower initial payments). Maybe a new loan to cover a balloon is the answer. (We'll discuss all of these in subsequent chapters.) Whatever you suggest, the lender should be receptive. He or she should be anxious to go the whole nine yards to help you out. After all, if the lender helps you, he or she will in reality be helping himself or herself.

IF THE LENDER WON'T COOPERATE

On the other hand, maybe you've got a real hard-nosed lender. This lender might simply not realize what's to his or her advantage. The lender might have some other motive that you don't know about and can't find out. The lender might simply be unreachable by negotiation.

This doesn't happen often. But when it does, you may end up walking out of the lender's office with little more than you came in with (except you probably will have gained the respect of the lender).

If negotiation fails then it's time to take other positive steps. You have many options, some of which you've already discussed with the lender and others (as we will soon see) you haven't told the lender about. Now it's time to think about these.

But don't give up on negotiation. The lender might not believe you would really follow through on some of the things you've talked about. Once you actually file a lawsuit or go to court, the lender's whole attitude might change, and negotiation might again become a possibility.

NEVER GIVE UP ON NEGOTIATION

Many times you will find the best solution is to sell and move down to a smaller home. Ask the lender for time to do just that. Ask him or her to recommend a realtor that *he or she* feels can move the property fast. Call the lender every day with progress reports: "We had two people through yesterday. One may make an offer [etc.]. Keep calling until the lender says, "Hey, relax, I know you are trying. You don't need to call every day. Just call occasionally to keep in touch."

Even when your adversary seems immovable, be ready, willing, and open to negotiate. I recommend you read *You Can Negotiate Anything* by Herb Cohen.

Chapter Four
NEGOTIATING WITH A PRIVATE LENDER

"Never get angry. Never make a threat. Reason with people . . ."
—Don Corleone

Now let's consider negotiation when our lender happens to be not institutional, but rather a private person. There's a world of difference between buying a secondhand car from a used-car salesperson and buying one from a private individual. The salesperson wants a sale and usually doesn't care which car you buy. He or she has handled hundreds of buyers and knows the ins and outs of selling and closing. We might feel, usually with good reason, that we are being manipulated toward purchasing.

With a private seller, on the other hand, it's a different story. Normally the seller only has one car in which he or she has a personal investment. The seller probably doesn't have a lot of sales finesse or polish. We might have to do the manipulating in order to get the car.

Something similar happens with lenders. Institutional lenders have the financial and legal knowledge. They have the finesse that comes from dealing with borrowers on a regular basis. Private lenders don't. Perhaps more importantly, institutional lenders are dealing with other people's money. Private lenders are dealing with their own.

The point is that we have to treat private lenders differently from institutional lenders. If we go to a private lender and begin spouting about Regulation Z and using high pressure, we're going to alarm that private individual. He or she might think, "Boy, this borrower is a real threat. I'd better not negotiate at all. I'd better run to my attorney!"

That's probably not the reaction we want. Undoubtedly what we are looking for is cooperation, not confrontation.

(Note: Not all private lenders are unsophisticated. Some make a point of loaning large amounts on real estate. These lenders might be just as sophisticated as the institutional lender, and we shouldn't hesitate to use the techniques of the last chapter on them.)

GOALS

The private lender usually has goals that are different from those of the institutional lender. Although a banker might be concerned, for example, with cash flow, the private lender might be looking at retirement income or be very concerned about taxes and finding ways to defer income to reduce them.

When we talk with a private lender, therefore, we need to be far more goal oriented than with an institutional lender. With the banker we can assume what his or her goals are. With the private lender we need to probe to find those goals so that we can then use them to achieve our own objectives.

Let's take a look at how this might work:

We make an appointment with the individual who holds the second mortgage balloon on our house. As before, we go through the early steps of confirming our appointment to let this person know we're taking a businesslike approach.

Again as before, when we arrive we don't take a pity me attitude; rather, we talk about the fact that we are having difficulty meeting our balloon (or making our payments or whatever the problem is). We point out that foreclosure is a possibility and that we are sure it would be to *both* our advantages to avoid it. (If the lender doesn't know why it's to his or her advantage to avoid foreclosure, we explain about high costs, lost interest, difficulty in reselling, and other reasons we've discussed.)

Now we begin probing: "If I paid off this loan in full right now, would you have a specific use or need for that money?"

If the private lender answers yes, as nearly all do, we pursue and ask what that goal might be: The lender might reply, "I'd invest it in another home loan."

Here the investor is telling us two things. First, the investor is interested in keeping that money working for him or her by investing. Second, the investor has selected real estate as the medium for his or her investment.

Now we point out that if the investor is going to reinvest in real estate, why not reinvest with us in the current property? With us the investor has a known quantity. We've been making the payments regularly (if indeed we have) and the house is a good one (if indeed it is). We can save the investor time and lost interest if he or she will simply roll that balloon over for us.

A sensible investor will seriously consider this sensible proposal. Notice that we're not asking for something for nothing. We're simply pointing out benefits to the investor that will also benefit us. If the investor decides to roll the loan over, our balloon payment problems are solved.

On the other hand, perhaps the investor is hesitant to roll that loan over for us. Maybe we were late for a payment once or twice.

Now we might explain the extenuating circumstances that caused us to be late. We might also say we are willing to have a five percent per month late fee included in the new mortgage (if one isn't already included in the old mortgage). By thus explaining and sweetening the pot, we might convince a hesitant private lender to roll over the mortgage.

But perhaps the lender is still hesitant.

Our solution might be to sweeten the pot even more. If the lender will roll the loan over for another three years, for instance, we'll agree to increase the interest rate by one or two percent. It's hard to find a private lender who won't listen to this argument.

But perhaps our lender has been listening to us sweeten the pot and is now wondering where we'll stop. Maybe if he or she continues saying no we'll continue sweetening. If that happens, it's time to get back to discussing the other alternative, foreclosure, and the problems that means for the lender.

Reinvesting the money is only one goal a private lender might have. When we ask about others our lender might scratch his or her chin and say, "I have a special use for that money."

"Oh really," we inquire, "What could that be?"

We now must devote our energies to getting the private lender to divulge what he or she wants to do with the money if we pay off the balloon mortgage in full.

Maybe our lender discloses that he or she really wants the money to put into a tax-deferred IRA or KEOGH account. Each month when we make a payment, the interest is taxable income to our private lender. If we pay off, the lender can deposit (up to certain limits) in a KEOGH or IRA plan and take a tax deduction for the deposit. In addition, any money earned while in the plan will not be immediately taxable.

Now we have several options. We might point out that there are limits to the amount a person can deposit in a single year in IRAs (about 2,000 dollars) or KEOGHs (the smaller of 15,000 dollars or fifteen percent of income). If our mortgage is for more than the private lender can deposit in a single year, would the lender consider a balloon payment of just the amount he or she can deposit? We would continue making payments on the balance and give the lender a second payment for deposit to his or her plan next year and so on.

In this fashion we might be able to significantly reduce the *amount* of the balloon payment we have coming due.

On the other hand, we might not be able to pay any of the balloon. In this case we might ask the lender just how much he or she is paying in taxes on our monthly payment. Usually the lender is angry about taxes and happy to say how much he or she is paying.

Now we can offer to increase our monthly payment to the point where we in effect cover the lender's tax liability. If our payment, for example, were 100 dollars per month, we might offer to double it to 200 dollars per month (increasing the interest rate accordingly). We offer this for a period of six or twelve months or however long a breather we need to arrange for other financing, to sell the property, or to come up with another solution. There aren't many lenders who'll pass up this offer.

Of course, private lenders have many diverse goals. There was one case where a lender was using the money he received on his mortgage to make payments on a houseboat. If the borrower didn't make the mortgage payments on the house, the lender couldn't make the payments on the houseboat.

Once the borrower understood the lender's goals, the borrower pointed out that foreclosure was not a good answer. It would mean that the lender wouldn't get his payments for as long as six to twelve months while the foreclosure process was underway, and that could mean the loss of the houseboat.

As a compromise, the lender agreed to *help* the borrower out. The lender offered his good credit to help the borrower secure a *new* loan on the house. With this money the private lender's mortgage was paid off (and he was able to pay off the houseboat). Our borrower had a new, longer-term mortgage plus some cash to work with (the refinance turned out to be for more than the original loan.)

Our goal in determining the private lender's goal is to get a handle on what that person's financial objective is. Once we know, we can think creatively about a solution that will benefit both of us. Until we know the private lender's goal, however, we really have no chance to solve our problem.

When all else fails, cry. When you have exhausted reason and it appears there is no hope, make an *emotional appeal*. Take your spouse and children to the lender's home or office and have them cry. Remember, your future happiness may depend on your emotional appeal to the lender.

If you have a private lender who is married, your odds of success will improve dramatically if you go to their house with your spouse. I know this from firsthand experience.

THE BOTTOM LINE

The bottom line is that one of the best ways of solving the problem of foreclosure is to deal directly with the lender.

I want to make it clear, however, that talking with the lender is not a single-time occurrence. We don't just talk with the lender when we first get into problems and then never talk to the lender again. *Talking with the lender is an ongoing process that occurs each step of the way out of foreclosure.*

Chapter Five
HOW TO MAKE YOUR LOAN CURRENT

"The meek shall inherit the earth—but not its mineral rights."
—J. Paul Getty

Facing foreclosure is like facing a war. We have to be ready to fight both tactically and strategically. In this chapter we're going to assume that our strategy is to save our home. Now we have to consider tactics. Our tactic here is to get our home out of foreclosure by paying up the amount we owe on our mortgage. If we can get our mortgage current, then we've pulled ourselves back from the brink of foreclosure.

FINDING OUT WHERE WE ARE FINANCIALLY

The first step in making our mortgage current is to get a realistic assessment of our current financial position. Of course, most of us think we already know the answer here.

Surprisingly, few of us really know at any given time where we are financially. To find out where we are we must get three pieces of paper.

On one piece of paper we list all our liabilities. This includes everything we owe including our current mortgage debt, any charge card loans, car payments—everything. (Note: We are not listing monthly payments here. What we are listing is the actual amount of the debt; for example, the full amount owed on the mortgage plus back payments, penalties, and interest.)

On the next piece of paper we list our assets. This includes our full house value, the value of our car, any loans owed us by others, cash on hand, cash coming in, and so forth.

Now we add up everything on the first sheet of paper and everything on the second and subtract the second total from the first. This will give us our current net value.

In most cases our current net value will be positive. That means that we have assets in excess of debts. If that's the case then it remains for us to figure out how to convert some of our assets into cash, which we can then use to make our mortgage current. (I'll give some suggestions on this later.)

On the other hand, it's just possible that we might have negative net value. That means that the amount we owe actually exceeds the amount we own. If this is the case, then we should seriously consider the option of bankruptcy. If we owe more than we own, it might not make sense to continue trying to salvage our home. Our situation might indeed be financially over the brink, and bankruptcy might be our best option.

Assuming that we do have a positive net value, we take our third and final sheet of paper and write "CASH FLOW" at the top. On this sheet we will list all of the cash that flows into and out of our hands each month.

On the left-hand side of the sheet we should list all of our sources of income. These include money from our job, money from incidentals such as selling small assets we might have, a motorcycle or old furniture, for instance, money from a second mortgage we might own and on which people are paying us, and so forth.

On the right-hand side of the sheet we should now list all of our expenses. These include payments for food, utilities, clothing, entertainment, and most important, the amount necessary to make our mortgage current.

(Note: In the last two chapters we discussed negotiating with the lender. Our lender, we hope, was receptive and has given us an extension of some sort under the terms of which we can pay back a certain amount each month until the mortgage is current. If that's the case, then we should list on the right-hand side of our sheet the current payback amount.

On the other hand, if our lender was intractable, we now have to figure out for ourselves how much time we have left to save our mortgage (refer to Chapter One) and how much money we need to raise. For example, to make our mortgage current we may need three months payments plus penalties. In terms of time left, we have two months in which to raise the amount. We now add three months payments plus the next two months plus penalties and divide by the remaining time, two months. This gives us the amount we have to raise in each of the next two months in order to save our mortgage.

Now we subtract the figures for outflow on the right side from the figures for income on the left side.

If we are extraordinarily lucky, we will be able to make this calculation. That is, the amount we have coming in will indeed cover the amount we owe including what's necessary to make our mortgage good. If that's the case, we simply wait until the money comes in, write the appropriate check, and our problem is solved.

MONTHLY CASH FLOW SHEET

CURRENT INCOME		CURRENT EXPENSES	
Source	$ amount	Source	$ amount
_____	_____	Variable _____	_____
_____	_____	_____	_____
_____	_____	_____	_____
_____	_____	Fixed _____	_____
_____	_____	_____	_____
_____	_____	_____	_____
Total $ _____		Total $ _____	

INCOME $ _____

Minus EXPENSES   − _____

SHORTFALL (or excess) $ _____

USING FINANCIAL KNOWLEDGE
TO GET OUT OF FORECLOSURE

In almost all cases, unfortunately, what we discover is that we have a negative cash flow situation. The amount on the left-hand side of the sheet is less than the amount we need to satisfy the right-hand side of the sheet. Our outflow is in excess of our income. If this is the case, then we must now determine exactly how much we are short. We subtract the left-hand side of our page from the right and come up with a figure. That's the amount we are short. That's the amount we need this month in order to make our mortgage current.

At this point we must now figure a way to increase our income or decrease our outflow. Let's consider the latter first:

DECREASING OUTFLOW

Decreasing outflow really comes down to calculation and sacrifice. Calculation means determining which expenses are fixed and which are variable.

Fixed expenses include such items as the amount necessary to make the mortgage current, taxes, car payments, credit card payments, and similar terms.

Variable expenses include everything else. They are the expenses for food, clothing, entertainment, and so forth.

Now we come to sacrifice. Sacrifice means determining how much we are willing to give up in order to cut down enough on our expenses to have the money to make the mortgage current. Sacrifice starts with variable expenses. For this and the next month we can eat nothing but cereal and peanut butter sandwiches. We can save on our food expenses. We can buy no new clothes. We can avoid going out entirely.

By thus sacrificing we can hope to cut down our expenses somewhat. We can actually calculate the amount we can save in this process. If it happens to be enough to cover our shortfall, then our problems are solved.

Usually, however, the amount we owe for the next few months is still in excess of the amount we've saved by our sacrifice. If that's the case then additional sacrifice is necessary. One way for this is to convert fixed expenses to variable expenses.

We might consider not making the utility payment or not making the carry payment or not making some other *must* payment.

This involves risk. We could have our gas or electricity turned off. Our car could be repossessed. On the other hand, maybe we could talk to the utility company and the car loan company and explain that we are having difficult times. Could they wait a month or two for payment? We could try to negotiate with them. Perhaps we could gain some time and use it, so to speak, to rob Peter to pay Paul.

Even if we are able to do this, we might find that we still can't raise enough money to cover our shortfall. In other words, no matter how much we sacrifice, we can't cut our expenses sufficiently to raise the money we need. What do we do now?

INCREASING INCOME

When we can't cut expenses, we have to increase income. There are basically only two ways to increase income.

First, we can seek new ways to gain income. This can include taking a part-time job, borrowing from relatives or friends, or getting someone who owes us money to pay sooner than scheduled.

Second, we can sell or borrow on some of our assets. You'll recall that we already figured out what our net worth was. Assuming our net worth is greater than our cash flow shortfall, our problem now is how to convert that net worth into cash that we can use to pay back the mortgage.

Some of the methods for this include selling a boat, a car, or a motorcycle we own, selling furniture, selling our favorite fishing gear (remember, I told you this involved sacrifice!), and selling any other assets we have.

We could also borrow against our assets. We could get a new car loan. We could go to a finance company or a bank and try to get another mortgage on our home.

This last course is often the quickest and the easiest, though not necessarily the best. Getting cash against our home is easy, *if* our equity is big enough. Some lenders don't care what our financial situation is. They don't care if we're employed or out of work, if we're in foreclosure or otherwise having difficulties. All they care about is that we have equity in our house. They will lend to us on the basis of that equity alone—the house becomes the full collateral. (These lenders always advertise in the newspapers and the Yellow Pages.)

The problem here is that they frequently charge very high interest rates or add points (percentages of the loan charged just to obtain it) and have short payback periods. By borrowing in this way we might actually end up just postponing our problem. Yes, we might get enough to pull us out of foreclosure now. But the added payments might be such a burden that within six months we'll be back in foreclosure, only then we'll owe on one more mortgage.

On the other hand, what we might need is time. With time we might be able to slim down our expenses, increase our income, and otherwise make ourselves battle ready so that in the future we won't find ourselves in the current credit crunch.

THE BOTTOM LINE

The bottom line is that if we have a greater net worth than the amount we need to get our mortgage current, we probably can bail ourselves out. The key is our being willing to make sacrifices.

AVOIDING MISTAKES

Ultimately the best results are going to come from clear thinking. What we want to do is to avoid making the mistakes that cause foreclosure. Here are five steps that drive people into losing their home. Are you guilty of any of them?

FIVE STEPS TO LOSING YOUR HOME
1. Don't read the documents.
2. Don't answer letters or phone calls from lenders.
3. Wait, wait, wait for your ship to come in.
4. Don't figure out your financial position and options.
5. Be dogmatic and closed-minded.

If you find yourself anywhere on the above list, watch out. You could be a prime candidate for losing your home!

Chapter Six
CREDIT AND YOU

"If you keep on doing the same old thing in the same old way you'll be the same old broke."

Credit is a problem for most of us. Although getting it might be easy, using it wisely can be very difficult. It is the misuse of credit that often gets us into foreclosure.

In this chapter we're going to look at credit from two perspectives. On one hand, we're going to be concerned with how to use credit wisely so that we don't get into foreclosure. On the other hand, we're going to consider credit protections that we may use once we are already in foreclosure.

One of the best ways to avoid future credit problems (before foreclosure) is to keep track of our money.

Most of us do not spend money only once a month. We spend it daily in many forms. We pay cash for some items. For others we write checks. For still others we use a credit card. If we're having trouble making our expenses meet our income, then we are in the position of being too "money fat." We have to lose weight. Just as dieters find that keeping track of what they eat and when they eat it helps them to control their intake, so will keeping track of what we spend and where we spend it allow us to control our expenses.

To do this we need two things. The first is time. At a set time once each month we pay all bills and we apportion all money for expenses. One handy way to do this is to use envelopes. We get a bunch of envelopes. Into one we put all our money for food. Into another goes money for clothes. A third holds money for utilities, and so forth. When the money for a particular use is gone, when the envelope is empty, we don't spend any more money on that.

Another useful item to have is a small, inexpensive notebook. In that notebook we write down everything we buy. Before we buy a new stereo cartridge or that great shirt, we must make a note in our notebook. If we have to account for our purchase in our little notebook, we'll probably think twice before buying. That notebook will remind us each time that we're facing foreclosure, now or sometime in the future, and maybe we'll hold off making the purchase.

Finally, we need realistic credit goals. Again, this is like losing weight. I once knew a man who wanted to lose weight. His method was simple. He said, "For the next year I'm not going to eat any candy or cookies." He ended up losing about two pounds per month and by the end of the year, he was at his desired weight.

We can do something similar. We can, for example, cut up all our credit cards. From that moment forward, we'll pay cash only. We won't charge anything. If we can't pay cash, we'll go without.

The point is that our credit goals must be realistic. We can't hope to survive financially if we set goals that we fail to meet. But if we set small, realistic goals and meet them, we will succeed in getting out of and avoiding future foreclosure.

HOW TO GET CREDIT HELP

If we're faced with foreclosure, it's a good guess that we are candidates for help. One of the best ways to get help is to contact one of the several consumer financial aid organizations. One such organization is the National Foundation for Consumer Credit (NFCC).

The NFCC is a national organization with offices in most major cities. Its goal is to help consumers straighten out their financial credit situation. They provide counselors who help consumers to help themselves.

A person going to the NFCC will find that he or she can meet with an experienced financial counselor who will analyze the situation and then suggest ways of handling the debt. A plan can be created for dealing with debt and the counselor may even help contact the creditors and get them to go along with the plan.

Of course the service is not free, but the fees are usually reasonable. Since the NFCC is funded primarily by donations, the fee really covers only a small part of the actual cost.

The NFCC is open to all who need credit counseling. This runs the gamut from the rich to the poor. A person who makes 150,000 dollars per year but spends 200,000 dollars might actually be in greater need of help than a person who makes 10,000 dollars and spends 12,000 dollars.

Local units of the NFCC are usually found under the title of Consumer Credit Counseling Service. (Look in the white pages of your phone book.) The national address is: National Foundation for Consumer Credit, 1819 H Street, N.W., Washington, D.C. 20006.

A similar organization is the Family Service Association of America, 44 East 23rd Street, New York, NY 10010. It also has numerous offices nationwide.

CREDIT RIGHTS

Over the past decade, at all levels of government (federal, state, and local), special protections have been set up to help consumers with credit. Most of these protections apply principally to credit card and retail purchases, but many also apply to mortgages. (We'll see the bigger implications of this when we discuss Regulation Z.)

Perhaps the most helpful agency is the Federal Trade Commission (FTC). The FTC has the authority to protect the consumer from both unfair credit (giving you unfair terms when you get credit) as well as unfair and deceptive practices in foreclosure.

The FTC has the right to protect a borrower from a lender who is threatening foreclosure in several ways. These include protecting the consumer from a creditor who *threatens* in a deceptive manner. This could be sending false documents or letters that look official or bear a resemblance to governmental papers. Sometimes to intimidate a borrower, a lender may send a document that looks like a summons. In fact it might not be, but it has the effect of strong intimidation. The FTC has the authority to step in and take action against a lender in such a case.

The lender may not threaten you with action unless the lender intends taking that action. The lender can't say he or she is going to take you to court unless he or she fully does intend to do so. (In most cases of a trust deed, *no court action is initiated by the lender.*)

Most lenders, particularly today, have a collection department. Sometimes this department is staffed with personnel whose goal is to get the mortgage payment from you any way they can. This might include calling up your employer and notifying him or her that you are a deadbeat and aren't making your mortgage payment. As a borrower, you have the right to take legal action if the lender inflicts emotional distress on you. You may even have the right to charge extortion, depending on the kind of threats used.

THE PROBLEM

The difficulty with all of the rights just mentioned is that there probably isn't going to be someone around to press your case for you. You'll probably need an attorney. The attorney will need to write letters to the mortgage lender for you and if necessary, press your action in court. (Sometimes just a letter from an attorney, however, will show some lenders you mean business and might make negotiating a lot easier.)

EQUAL CREDIT OPPORTUNITY ACT

There are other rights that you as a borrower have under the Equal Credit Opportunity Act. Most of these, however, apply primarily when you obtain the mortgage, not later on when you are faced with foreclosure. Basically the lender may not discriminate because of the sex or the marital status of the borrower. The act also includes prohibitions against discrimination on the basis of age, race, color, religion, or being a welfare recipient.

FAIR CREDIT REPORTING ACT

This protects us against erroneous or unfair credit reporting. It is vital to protecting our credit when we're faced with foreclosure.

Even if we make our mortgage good or even if we've taken steps to insure that our credit is not blemished by a foreclosure, we might find that the foreclosure is reported by a reporting agency. If that's the case, we might want to take action to have the false report removed. In so doing it is important to understand that our rights include.

1. the right to know which reporting agency issued a report that denied us credit

2. the right to know the nature, substance, and source (except investigative reports) of any derogatory information (except information of a medical nature)

3. the right to take a friend of our own choosing with us and to go to the reporting agency to get information

4. the right to have erroneous or incomplete information reinvestigated and changed

5. the right to include our own version of what happened in the credit report

6. the right to have those who previously received erroneous or incomplete information notified of the changes

There are numerous other rights that the Fair Credit Reporting Act specifically provides to the borrower. Unfortunately, it does not allow us either to get a copy of a credit report on ourselves or to see the reporting agency's file on us.

Nevertheless, should a foreclosure appear on a credit report after we have transferred title *prior* to foreclosure, or should a report of a notice of default appear on a credit report after we have corrected the default, we can take steps under this act to correct the report.

It is worth noting, however, the limitations of this act. It does not empower the FTC to help us out specifically if we have a problem. The FTC can investigate and bring action against an agency for unfair reporting, but that probably won't help us personally. To get a bad credit report changed we might have to go so far as to hire an attorney and even press a lawsuit against the reporting agency (assuming our own personal nudging and hollering doesn't get the desired results).

Credit is something we all need in today's world. It is important to remember that credit is not bad. It is the *misuse* of credit that is the enemy.

Chapter Seven
GETTING AN FHA LOAN EXTENSION

"The one permanent emotion of the inferior man, as of all the simpler mammals, is fear—fear of the unknown, the complex, the inexplicable."
—H.L. Mencken

Over the past forty years millions and millions of homes have been financed using FHA (Federal Housing Administration) insurance. If your home mortgage happens to be an FHA loan, you may have a lot more options than you thought when you are faced with foreclosure. The FHA offers borrowers a lot of second chances to make good their loans. The problem is that you have to know about the opportunities to take advantage of them.

DO YOU HAVE AN FHA-INSURED MORTGAGE?

Remember, the only borrowers who will be able to take advantage of the benefits I'm going to describe are those who have FHA loans. The first step, therefore, is to determine what kind of financing you have on your home.

An FHA loan does not mean the money was borrowed from the FHA. Instead, at the time of purchase, the house and the buyer met strict FHA qualifications, and because they met them, the FHA agreed to insure the loan. (This means that in the event you don't make your payments, the actual lender will have the loan made good by the FHA.)

Since the FHA didn't lend the money, you aren't paying your monthly payments directly to the FHA. You might be paying them to a bank, a savings and loan, or even a mortgage company. To find out if you do indeed have an FHA loan (in case you don't know), you can check with the lender. A quicker method is to check your monthly loan card. If it includes a one-half percent charge for FHA insurance, you have an FHA mortgage.

WHY THE FHA HELPS

As I've pointed out earlier, institutional lenders do not want to take back property. That, in fact, is the last thing that a lender wants. In an FHA-insured mortgage, the bank that loaned the money has an option if we are in foreclosure. Instead of taking the property back itself, it can turn the mortgage over to the insurer. The bank gets its cash, and the FHA gets the house.

But the FHA doesn't want the house any more than the bank did. It's in business to insure mortgages, not to own houses. The FHA makes a great effort to try to keep from getting houses back in foreclosure. (In addition, since it is a governmental organization, it strives to help the borrower in any way it can.)

In order to understand how the FHA helps, it's first necessary to understand how it operates. The FHA, although it is a governmental organization, receives no money from the government. It is self-funding. That one-half percent in mortgage insurance that borrowers pay funds the entire program.

When there are a lot of foreclosures, as there are during a deep recession, the FHA fund is overloaded. It could take back tens of thousands of properties, thereby draining off money from the fund.

THE FHA EXTENSION

To prevent this from happening, the FHA, through its parent agency, the Department of Housing and Urban Development

(HUD), has created a plan to aid borrowers on FHA loans who get into trouble.

The big problem with the plan, however, is publicity. Very few people know about it. It isn't automatically offered. A borrower has to take several specific steps in order to get under the plan.

The bail out program is available *only* to those borrowers who have FHA loans. If you have a VA (Veterans Administration) or a conventional loan, this will not benefit you. You must have an FHA loan to benefit here.

The bail out works in this fashion. If you have defaulted (not made the monthly payment) on your FHA mortgage, *you can ask the Department of Housing and Urban Development to take over your mortgage.*

This is a vital step. It is not automatic. Remember, you have a mortgage from a lender such as a bank or a savings and loan association. If you don't make payments, that lender will start foreclosure. The foreclosure procedure usually will continue until, ultimately, you lose your house. Once the lender has title to your property, it will then transfer it to the FHA (HUD).

But that's too late for you. You will have already lost your property. What you must do the moment you default is *request an immediate transfer of title from the lender to HUD.*

In this, HUD now becomes the lender, and you can apply for the bail out program.

HOW TO DO IT

To start the process, the borrower has to contact any of the HUD offices. They are located in nearly every major city, and the head office is in Washington, D.C. (Look in your phone book or call Washington directory information.)

Once you've contacted HUD, you'll find that it has at least three criteria you must meet for determining whether or not it will take over your mortgage and let you into the bail out program.

The criteria are:

> 1. You must be behind in your payments. Usually you must be behind at least three payments. Being behind fewer than three usually disqualifies a borrower from consideration. Being behind more than three will not disqualify a borrower from consideration.

2. You must have a *good reason* for having missed the payments. HUD has strict rules about what constitutes good reasons. For example, if you took on more debt than you could handle and then found that you could not make your monthly payments, you might not qualify. The reason would be that it was *your choice* to take on the debt. You could easily have decided not to act. The criteria here is that if you can't make the payments because you got yourself into trouble, you shouldn't ask HUD to bail you out.

The reasons for not making payments must be something beyond your own control. This would include being laid off from work (but not necessarily quitting voluntarily or being fired for good cause). Another common reason usually considered sufficient is illness. Perhaps you broke a leg and couldn't work for four months. Presumably the injury was beyond your control and so you would qualify.

An illness, however, must be *limited.* That is, if you couldn't make your payments because you were permanently paralyzed without any hope of recovery, then you probably wouldn't qualify unless you could get a friend or a relative to agree to resume payments at the end of a period of time if you couldn't.

3. Finally, there must be a reasonable expectation of your being able to make your payments again within a specific period of time. For example, perhaps you had a heart attack and were forced to stay home from work for six months. Presumably at the end of six months you could work again. If that were the case, then you would have a reasonable prospect of being able to earn the money necessary to make your payments within a reasonable length of time.

One big reason for not being able to make payments is being laid off from work. How does someone who has been laid off demonstrate a reasonable prospect of being able to make regular payments?

There are a number of ways. The best way, of course, is to show that you've been rehired. If you only need time to catch up and you already have a job, then you're halfway home.

Another way is to show that you are enrolled in a training program and will be able to start a job as soon as the training ends. Typically HUD will allow up to a year for the training as long as a reasonable prospect of a job can be seen at the end of that time.

These then are the three basic criteria that HUD uses to evaluate whether or not it will grant a borrower a bail out. But just what is this HUD bail out?

The bail out is a loan extension. It is typically handled in this fashion. After the mortgage has been transferred to HUD, the borrower meets with a HUD counselor. The counselor looks at the prospects and the qualifications of the borrower. If the counselor decides that the borrower has all the qualifications, then a plan is arranged for repaying the loan so that it will become current within *three years*. In other words, the bail out involves extending the payback period for a maximum of three years.

The actual terms of the extension depend on each borrower's individual situation. They could mean making half-payments for several years, then paying higher payments until the mortgage is caught up; or they could mean no payments for as much as eighteen months, then double payments for eighteen months until the mortgage is caught up.

The bail out is an individualized plan. HUD works with each borrower to tailor a program that the borrower can live with.

In addition, once the plan is approved, HUD also gives the borrower a list of HUD-approved agencies that specialize in financial counseling and can give additional aid in avoiding foreclosure in the borrower's particular situation.

All in all the HUD bail out is one of the best deals going in the marketplace today. But remember, it's not a gift, and it doesn't happen automatically. You as the borrower have to apply to get it.

To summarize, here are the steps to be taken to get an FHA bail out:

Step One: Determine if you have an FHA mortgage.

Step Two: Contact HUD and see if your mortgage can be transferred.

Step Three: Qualify for the bail out program under the three basic criteria:

1. at least three months behind in payments
2. have a good reason for not making payments (as defined by HUD)
3. have a reasonable expectation of being able to make the loan current within a maximum of three years

Step Four: Work out an individual bail out plan with HUD.

THE BAIL OUT ACCORDING TO HUD

In doing research for this book I obtained a copy of the Housing and Urban Development (HUD) *Handbook on Administration of the Home Mortgage Program*. Here are some points of interest directly from the handbook (I have added the italics in most cases):

WAIVER OF RESIDENCY

Field Offices may now waive both the requirement that the mortgage property be the principal residence of the mortgagor and the requirement that the mortgagee not own other property subject to an FHA-insured or Secretary-held mortgage. When evaluating a mortgagor's ability to pay the mortgage in full or when structuring payment plans on mortgages accepted for assignment, the Field Office may extend the mortgage term by up to 10 years.

ELIGIBILITY CRITERIA [to give forbearance]

[Note: Portions of text are omitted.]

a. The mortgagee must have indicated to the mortgagor its intention to foreclose the mortgage.

b. At least three full monthly payments due on the mortgage are unpaid after allowance for any partial payments which may have been accepted and not yet credited to the account. . . .

d. *The default must have been caused by a circumstance or set of circumstances beyond the mortgagor's control which temporarily rendered the family financially unable to cure the delinquency within a reasonable time or make full mortgage payments.*

e. *There must be a reasonable prospect that the mortgagor will be able to resume full mortgage payments after a temporary period of reduced or suspended payments, not exceeding 36 months, and will be able to pay the mortgage in full by its original maturity date extended, if necessary, by up to ten years.* Future ability to pay—not present income or credit history—is the key factor in evaluating this criterion. No applicant for assignment shall be determined ineligible based simply upon lack or type of income at the time the assignment request is processed.

The HUD bail out is one of the best programs around. If you have an FHA loan, don't overlook it.

Assignment Procedures
Flow Chart

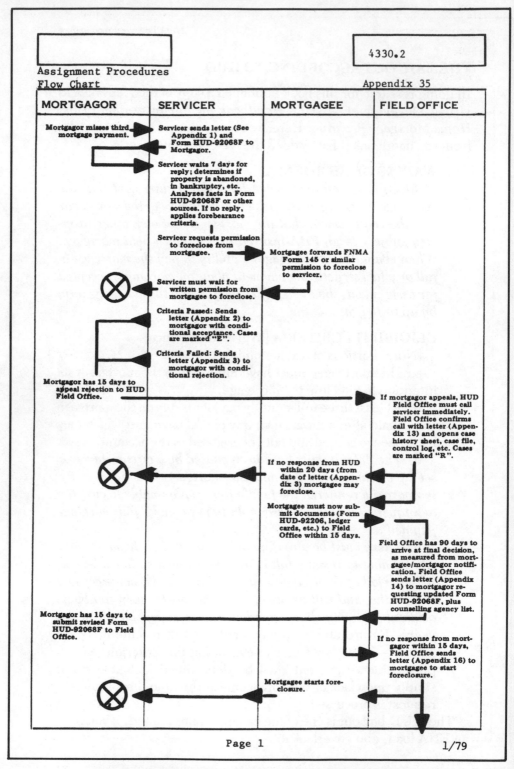

MORTGAGOR	SERVICER	MORTGAGEE	FIELD OFFICE

Mortgagor misses third mortgage payment.

Servicer sends letter (See Appendix 1) and Form HUD-92068F to Mortgagor.

Servicer waits 7 days for reply; determines if property is abandoned, in bankruptcy, etc. Analyzes facts in Form HUD-92068F or other sources. If no reply, applies forebearance criteria.

Servicer requests permission to foreclose from mortgagee.

Mortgagee forwards FNMA Form 145 or similar permission to foreclose to servicer.

Servicer must wait for written permission from mortgagee to foreclose.

Criteria Passed: Sends letter (Appendix 2) to mortgagor with conditional acceptance. Cases are marked "E".

Criteria Failed: Sends letter (Appendix 3) to mortgagor with conditional rejection.

Mortgagor has 15 days to appeal rejection to HUD Field Office.

If mortgagor appeals, HUD Field Office must call servicer immediately. Field Office confirms call with letter (Appendix 13) and opens case history sheet, case file, control log, etc. Cases are marked "R".

If no response from HUD within 20 days (from date of letter (Appendix 3) mortgagee may foreclose.

Mortgagee must now submit documents (Form HUD-92206, ledger cards, etc.) to Field Office within 15 days.

Field Office has 90 days to arrive at final decision, as measured from mortgagee/mortgagor notification. Field Office sends letter (Appendix 14) to mortgagor requesting updated Form HUD-92068F, plus counselling agency list.

Mortgagor has 15 days to submit revised Form HUD-92068F to Field Office.

If no response from mortgagor within 15 days, Field Office sends letter (Appendix 16) to mortgagee to start foreclosure.

Mortgagee starts foreclosure.

ASSIGNMENT PROCEDURE FLOW CHARTS

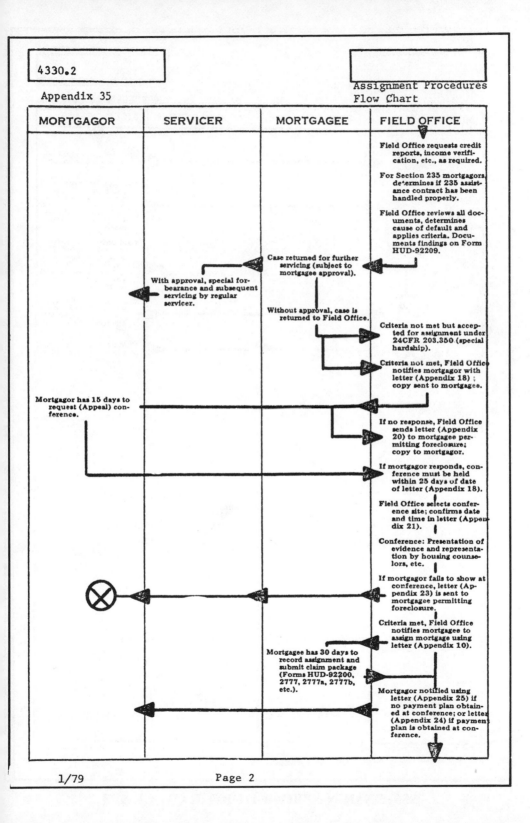

4330.2

Appendix 35

MORTGAGOR	SERVICER	MORTGAGEE	FIELD OFFICE

Field Office requests credit reports, income verification, etc., as required.

For Section 235 mortgagor, determines if 235 assistance contract has been handled properly.

Field Office reviews all documents, determines cause of default and applies criteria. Documents findings on Form HUD-92209.

Case returned for further servicing (subject to mortgagee approval).

With approval, special forbearance and subsequent servicing by regular servicer.

Without approval, case is returned to Field Office.

Criteria not met but accepted for assignment under 24CFR 203.350 (special hardship).

Criteria not met, Field Office notifies mortgagor with letter (Appendix 18) ; copy sent to mortgagee.

Mortgagor has 15 days to request (Appeal) conference.

If no response, Field Office sends letter (Appendix 20) to mortgagee permitting foreclosure; copy to mortgagor.

If mortgagor responds, conference must be held within 25 days of date of letter (Appendix 18).

Field Office selects conference site; confirms date and time in letter (Appendix 21).

Conference: Presentation of evidence and representation by housing counselors, etc.

If mortgagor fails to show at conference, letter (Appendix 23) is sent to mortgagee permitting foreclosure.

Criteria met, Field Office notifies mortgagee to assign mortgage using letter (Appendix 10).

Mortgagee has 30 days to record assignment and submit claim package (Forms HUD-92200, 2777, 2777a, 2777b, etc.).

Mortgagor notified using letter (Appendix 25) if no payment plan obtained at conference; or letter (Appendix 24) if payment plan is obtained at conference.

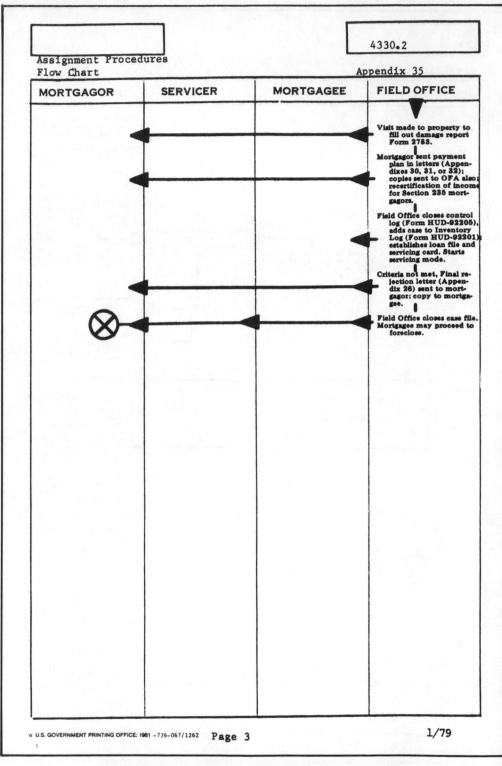

MORTGAGOR	SERVICER	MORTGAGEE	FIELD OFFICE

Visit made to property to fill out damage report Form 2783.

Mortgagor sent payment plan in letters (Appendixes 30, 31, or 32); copies sent to OFA also; recertification of income for Section 235 mortgagors.

Field Office closes control log (Form HUD-92205), adds case to Inventory Log (Form HUD-92201); establishes loan file and servicing card. Starts servicing mode.

Criteria not met, Final rejection letter (Appendix 26) sent to mortgagor; copy to mortgagee.

Field Office closes case file. Mortgagee may proceed to foreclose.

ASSIGNMENT PROCEDURE FLOW CHART

Chapter Eight
REFINANCING
OUT OF FORECLOSURE

"If you are able to state a problem, it can be solved."

It would be wonderful if when the old loan goes sour, we could solve the problem by getting a new loan.

Of course, as most of us realize, in today's market refinancing is a burden. It is difficult if not impossible for many homeowners to find refinancing at acceptable interest rates.

With some creative thinking, however, it may indeed be possible for you to refinance your property and save it from foreclosure. In this chapter we're going to look at the many financing alternatives that are available today.

First, let's get our definitions straight. When I say refinancing, I'm talking about getting a new first mortgage. (Obtaining a new second mortgage or other forms of financing are covered in other chapters.)

The reasons for the refinance can be varied. We might be facing foreclosure because of a balloon payment, because the current payments are too high, because we're unable to meet current payments due to unemployment, or because of other reasons. Regardless of *why* we want to refinance, we see obvious benefits.

The key to getting a refinance is the restructuring of our debt. It's turning in our old "first" for a new "first."

AMOUNT

Typically in a refinance we get additional amounts of money. Instead of owing, for example, 50,000 dollars, we end up owing 60,000 dollars. But we use the 10,000-dollar difference to pay off a balloon "second," or we get longer to pay. Instead of having a balance of, for example, seventeen years left on our mortgage, we refinance and get a mortgage that has forty years to run. The longer term reduces our payments. We can also get a different kind of mortgage, one that has lower payments at the beginning of its term and higher payments later on.

The type of loan that we get depends entirely on what the lender has to offer.

SOURCES

At this point, we shouldn't think that we *must* go to the holder of our existing mortgage to refinance. That is only one source, but usually it is a good source because the existing lender has a vested interest in the property. If the lender we have isn't cooperative, however, then we can feel free to seek out any other lender at all. The field is wide open. There are nearly 10,000 different banks and savings and loans to choose from in the United States, and money is money.

TYPES OF LOANS

The real thrust of this chapter is to explain the different types of loans we can expect to get from a lender. In today's market, variety is the rule, and we as borrowers have a great variety of refinancing to choose from.

First of all, here's a little bit of background. In the past, there was only one kind of mortgage—a fixed-rate, fixed-term loan. If we got the mortgage for, say, eight percent, that was the interest rate for the life of the loan. If it was for thirty years, then that was the term. There was no need to renegotiate the term. The interest rate did not fluctuate.

This type of loan is the best but increasingly difficult to find today. Now we have loans where the interest rate goes up or down, depending upon interest rates in general. In many cases, the term of the loan is renegotiated every five years or so. In other words, in today's market, we find great flexibility, which favors lenders.

Nevertheless, among all the various types of loans that are available, here are ten options we can choose from. (Note: Some lenders will have five or six, others one or two. We have to shop around to find the loan we think will be best for us.)

Type of Mortgage	Interest Rate	Term	Payments
fixed rate	market rate	usually 30 years	fixed
adjustable rate (ARM; also called variable interest rate [VIR]; or variable rate)	fluctuates	usually 30 years	variable

These mortgages have their interest rate indexed to a market rate such as the rate for six-month T-bills (treasury bills). Usually, as an inducement to get them, the starting rate might be a half-percent lower than the fixed rate. But the rate can soar when interest rates in general move up. There is no limit (usually) on the monthly payment. It can literally double overnight. In those cases where increases in the monthly payment are a part of the mortgage, the interest not collected in a forced low monthly payment is added to the mortgage, resulting in negative amortization. In other words, we end up owing more each month and paying interest on interest. These are not great loans but what's mostly available today.

Type of Mortgage	Interest Rate	Term	Payments
renegotiable rate (RRM)	fixed for 3-5 years	3-5 years but with a 30-year amortization	fixed for 3-5 years

In this type of mortgage, the borrower locks in a fixed interest rate, but only for a relatively short period of time—three to five years. During that time, the interest rate and the payment remain stable. (The loan payment is written as if the term were a full thirty years.) When the term expires after three to five years, the loan is rewritten by the lender at the interest rates then prevailing. In almost all cases, the lender agrees in advance to rewrite the loan—that is, we don't end up with a balloon.

87

Type of Mortgage	Interest Rate	Term	Payments
graduated payment (GPM)	fixed	30-40 years	move up

In this type of mortgage, the interest rate is fixed at the time the mortgage is obtained. The payment schedule is arranged, however, so that in the early years a low payment is made and in the later years a higher payment is made. This loan is usually advertised for young couples. The assumption is that when they are getting started, they can only afford a small amount in monthly payments, but as they get older and advance in their occupations, they will be able to afford higher payments. The difference between the initial payment and the later payments can be as much as one-third higher.

shared appreciation (SAM)	fixed	fixed	fixed

The SAM was the brainchild of several lenders during the big inflation period of the late 1970s. The idea was that in return for a lower interest rate (often two-thirds of the market rate), the lender would participate in the profits when the property was sold. For example, instead of getting a market rate of 12 percent on our mortgage, it might be only 8 percent (an inducement). When we sold, however, instead of getting 100 percent of the profits, we'd only get two-thirds, giving the other third to the lender. The trouble with this is that there haven't been many profits in sales recently and almost no lenders are offering SAMs.

balloons	fixed	fixed	last payment much higher

In the past, most institutional lenders could not offer balloon payments, but recent legislation has changed all that. Today balloons can be obtained from many banks and savings and loans. Under this kind of mortgage, we have a fixed monthly payment for ten, twenty, or even thirty years. But at the end of that time, we don't have the mortgage paid off; rather, we end up owing a big payoff. This is almost identical to the balloons we have with second mortgages.

Type of Mortgage	Interest Rate	Term	Payments
Federal Housing Administration	fixed or adjustable	fixed	fixed or graduated

(FHA)   An FHA loan is just like a fixed-rate or an adjustable loan. The difference is that the FHA sets the interest rate, usually about a half-point below the market rate. Because of this, there are usually points (percentages of the loan) to pay to the lender. (The buyer can only pay one point in a purchase.) Both the buyer and the home have to meet FHA qualifications, and the borrower pays an additional half-percent for FHA insurance.

| Veterans Administration (VA) | fixed | fixed | fixed or graduated |

This is usually available only to qualified veterans. The rate is close to market rate, and it is either a conventional fixed-rate loan or one with graduated payments. Both the house and the borrower must qualify to the VA, which guarantees payment.

| buy down | below market | fixed | fixed |

This type of loan is found almost exclusively today in new homes. A builder realizes that he or she can't sell houses because the current interest rate is too high. So the builder agrees to pay the lender a certain sum of money that will then be used to offset the interest rate. For example, the interest rate might be fifteen percent. But the builder will give the lender an amount of money equal to three percent of the mortgage, and thus the borrower (home buyer) ends up with an interest rate of only twelve percent. Typically, the costs here are so great that the buy down is only for one to three years. It can be, however, for the life of the loan if the builder is willing to put up the money.

| wraparound (wrap) | fixed | fixed | fixed |

A wrap is a device used to keep existing financing on the property. For example, instead of paying off the old low interest rate mortgage, the borrower receives a new mortgage that includes the old one. Payments are made on the new mortgage, and the lender of this new one then makes payments on the older mortgage to the old lender.

Refinancing today is bound to be a difficult game, simply because of the problems involved in finding a lender who will give you the kind of mortgage you want.

The best source for more information on financing in today's market is *The New Mortgage Game* by Robert Irwin (New York: McGraw-Hill Inc., 1982).

FANNIE MAE PRIVATE PURCHASES

Today there is an exciting new program for individuals who carried back financing on homes they sold. It can have a dramatic effect in clearing up a threatened balloon payment foreclosure or in getting monthly payments dramatically reduced.

Under this type of refinance we as the borrower have our *lender* refinance to us and then sell the new mortgage to Fannie Mae (Federal National Mortgage Association) for cash. We get a new (and better) mortgage. The lender gets the cash.

This is how it works:

After the mortgage has been made, the lender may sell it immediately or any time in the future to Fannie Mae. Fannie Mae is a quasi-governmental agency that acts as a secondary market for mortgage financing.

This gives the lender the knowledge and security of knowing that he or she can get cash by transferring the mortgage to Fannie Mae. In effect, this means that the lender will be less inclined to foreclose on a balloon and more willing to extend the term.

Alternately the lender could get the cash at the time of the balloon by rewriting it for a longer period and then selling to Fannie Mae. The borrower then simply repays Fannie Mae. The original lender, with cash, exits from the picture.

HOW TO GET IT

In order for a mortgage to qualify for purchase by Fannie Mae, it must meet strict criteria. These include the following:

1. The mortgage is usually either a first or a junior (second) mortgage.

2. The paperwork and the servicing (payment collection) must be handled by a Fannie Mae-approved mortgage service company. (A list of these may be obtained from Fannie Mae at HUD, Washington, D.C. 20410.)

3. The qualifying of the borrower and property must be approved *prior* to placing the loan on the property. The approval is handled by the mortgage service company.

Chapter Nine
SEVENTEEN WAYS TO HANDLE BALLOON PAYMENTS

"Some people wanted champagne and caviar when they should have had hot dogs and beer."
                                        —Dwight D. Eisenhower

One of the biggest problems faced by borrowers in America today is the balloon payment. This is without a doubt the one area where those who are capable of making monthly payments and are fairly well off financially still are threatened by the loss of their property. It's a real nightmare.

A balloon payment is usually defined as any one monthly payment that is more than two times higher than any other. For example, let's say we have a second mortgage as part of the purchase price of our home. That mortgage is for twelve percent interest on 10,000 dollars at 100 dollars per month, all due and payable in three years.

Now let's think about that for a minute. What is twelve percent per year interest on 10,000 dollars? If we take our calculator, we find out that it comes to 1,200 dollars. The interest alone is 1,200 dollars. Over the course of a year, that's 100 dollars per month.

Wait a minute, that's an interest-only loan!

That's right. Most "seconds" are indeed interest only or close to it.

Under the terms of this second mortgage, we pay 100 dollars per month for three years, and at the end of that time, we owe 10,000 dollars—exactly what we borrowed. That last payment of 10,000 dollars is called the balloon payment.

REASON FOR BALLOONS

Why would anybody in his or her right mind want a balloon payment? There are at least thirty different reasons why people have accepted balloon payments.

The big reason is that between 1979 and 1982 buying with a big "second" and a balloon payment was just about the only way that seventy percent of the home buyers could purchase. It was either buy with a "second" that carried a balloon or not buy at all. Besides, most people figured, within two or three years, the borrower would be able to refinance the property with a big, new, low interest rate first mortgage.

Of course, that didn't happen. Within a year or two of getting that balloon "second," mortgage interest rates were still high, money was scarce, and lenders were offering mainly adjustable-rate mortgages—ones that went up or down, depending on the rates of short-term money.

All of which meant that people who had bought with those big "seconds" suddenly found they were due. Now what to do? We've got a 10,000-, 20,000-, or 50,000-dollar mortgage that needs to be *paid off in full* coming due in a few months. If we don't pay it off, the lender is sure to declare us in default and foreclose on the property, taking it back. *What to do?*

THE ARAB AND THE SEVENTEEN CAMELS

At this point, I'm reminded of a certain story. Once there was an old Arab who did a very nasty thing. When he died he left a will that said his herd of camels was to be divided among his sons.

His eldest son was to receive *one-half* of his herd.

His middle son was to receive *one-third* of his herd.

His youngest son was to receive *one-ninth* of his herd.

The problem was that his herd consisted of seventeen camels. How do you divide seventeen in half? How do you divide it into thirds? How do you divide it into ninths?

Needless to say, the sons were upset about the old Arab's will. In fact, they were yelling, fighting, and carrying on when an old wise man, another Arab, happened by. He heard the commotion and went to ask what the trouble was.

Very quickly the sons explained the difficulty. The eldest son wanted his half, the middle son his third, and the youngest son his ninth. But the only way seemed to be to cut the camels up, and they didn't want dead camels. There was no solution.

The wise man smiled and said, "The answer is obvious. Here, I'll help you. I'll give you my camel."

The three sons looked at the old wise man in amazement. The man smiled and said, "Let me explain."

"When I give you my camel, your herd, which was seventeen camels, now has eighteen camels. With eighteen camels, we can make the following division:

"For the eldest son, who should receive half the herd, we divide eighteen in half and get nine camels. You take your nine camels."

The eldest son nodded and smiled. He certainly was getting half.

"For the middle son, who is to get a third, we divide eighteen by three and discover that it comes to six. You take your six camels."

The middle son smiled and took his camels. Indeed he was getting his rightful share.

"And for the youngest son, who is to receive a ninth, one-ninth of eighteen is two. You take your two camels."

The youngest son felt good, too. He had gotten what was due him.

"Now, the oldest has nine, the middle has six, and the youngest has two. Nine and six are fifteen and two comes to seventeen. That leaves one camel left over, which is mine."

At this point, the wise old man got back on his camel and rode off, leaving everyone feeling good.

Before you start scratching your head trying to figure how the wise old man did this, let me tell you what the story illustrates. It points out the fact that there's always room for a creative solution, if we look for it. On the other hand, if we get bogged down in our old set ways, we might never discover the answer to our problems. Just as the wise old man solved the riddle of the seventeen camels, so should we try to come up with a creative solution to foreclosure in the case of a balloon payment. To do this, here are a number of very helpful ideas.

Here's what you can do with a balloon payment mortgage that's coming due:

1. PLAN WELL IN ADVANCE

This is really the key to saving the property. If you wait until a few weeks before the balloon is due, you might indeed have a problem that can't be solved. On the other hand, if you start thinking about it a year or two in advance, then you may very well have time to come up with a solution.

Remember, when it comes to a balloon payment, there's nothing sudden or unexpected happening. We created this problem for ourselves when we agreed to a balloon at the time of purchase. If we have a balloon payment due in three years, then we have three years to prepare for its payment. We have three years to come up with a plan. We have three years to examine the market and our finances and learn what the best course of action to take is. The excuse that "I didn't have time to do anything" just won't wash with balloon payments. We do have the time, if we plan ahead.

2. TRY TO GET PAYMENT STAGING

One thing we might consider doing with a balloon is consider staging the payments so that they become more manageable. If we owe 10,000 dollars on a balloon payment that is coming due and we have to come up with it all at once, it might be fairly hard to make, depending on our finances and the money conditions in today's market.

On the other hand, if we can get the lender to agree to staging, then we might have a solution we can live with.

For example, let's say that long before the balloon is due (perhaps a year before), we go to the lender and explain that with the way the money market is currently, we don't think that we are going to refinance. But we don't want to lose the property. Would the lender agree to staging the balloon? Would he or she agree to take 3,000 dollars when the 10,000 dollars is due and then continue receiving payments on the balance for another year, when we would stage another payment of 3,000 dollars. We could continue this for one more year until we made the final payment of 4,000 dollars.

For the lender, this isn't such a terrible alternative to foreclosure. It means he or she will get the money—just not all at once. The lender will also be getting interest on the unpaid balance. At the same time, the lender won't be worried about having to go through foreclosure. The cost and uncertainty will be eliminated.

The advantage to us is obvious. We might not be able to raise 10,000 dollars in a single chunk, but we might be able to raise 3,000 dollars that way. (Of course, if thirty percent seems too high for us to raise, we could propose twenty percent, or ten, or whatever we could afford.) The idea is to get the holder of the mortgage to agree to staging the payments of the balloon. It's another way of getting our loan extended.

3. MAKE HIGHER PAYMENTS

What's the reason a balloon payment exists on a mortgage? The reason is that the monthly payments aren't high enough to pay the mortgage off.

But, if we plan ahead, what about making payments high enough to pay off the mortgage? On a mortgage of 10,000 dollars due in three years or thirty-six months, that's only 332 dollars per month *including interest* at twelve percent per year.

Think about it. On an interest-only mortgage such as the one just described, our payments would be 100 dollars per month. For just another 232 dollars per month more, we can get a fully amortized mortgage, one that is paid off at the end of the three-year period. If we can afford the higher payments, they surely are worthwhile.

A good alternative to this, when we can't make higher payments for the full three years or the term of the mortgage, is to offer the lender higher payments for the last year in exchange for delaying the payoff a year or more.

If the lender's goal happens to be cash flow, rather than a big chunk of cash all at once, the lender may jump at this. Instead of making payments of 100 dollars per month, as I already described, we make payments of 200 dollars per month for the last year in exchange for extending the loan an additional year. (In addition, the entire extra 100 dollars per month we are paying reduces the balance of the mortgage due on the balloon!)

4. USE THE BALLOON NOTE AS THE DOWN PAYMENT ON ANOTHER PROPERTY FOR THE LENDER

This is a very creative idea that may take a few minutes of your time to think about.

If the lender won't extend the term or stage payments, ask the lender what he or she wants to do with the balloon when it's paid off. What does the lender want to use the money for?

If the answer is that he or she plans to use the money to buy another house, then consider using the balloon mortgage as the down payment.

"What?" you may be saying. "How can a mortgage be used as a down payment?"

It's easy. In today's market, sellers are desperate to sell. Suppose a buyer comes to them and says, "I don't have cash to put down, but I have a mortgage owed me by another person. It's due in three years on another house. I'll use it as a down payment. I'll turn it over to you. You'll get payments each month and in three years, you'll collect your money in full with interest."

You don't think a seller anxious to sell will think seriously about this offer? I guarantee you one will.

What happens is that in exchange for using the balloon as a down payment on another house, the lender agrees to extend its term a few years more. You end up with a new lender and more time. The old lender ends up with what he or she wanted, another house. Both avoid the problems of foreclosure.

5. COLLATERALIZE THE BALLOON MORTGAGE

Collateral means putting up something of value in exchange for cash that you agree to pay back. As we've just seen, a mortgage with a balloon in it is collateral. It can be used as a down payment on a house. But as collateral, it can also be used for something else, namely getting cash from a bank or another lender.

Let's say that when we go to our lender to find out what he or she wants to do with the money from the balloon, the lender doesn't answer that he or she wants to buy another house, as was the case previously. Now the answer is that the lender needs some cash.

Okay, how do we get the lender cash for the balloon?

One way is for the lender on our mortgage to take the note to the bank and borrow on it. The lender can get the cash out that way.

But, of course, if the lender does that, he or she has to make payments.

How about if we make the payments for the lender? We agree to higher payments on the loan, high enough to cover both the amount we originally agreed to as well as the amount the lender has to pay to the bank under the terms of his or her borrowing. Higher payments, of course, make the note even better collateral.

We, on the other hand, say that what we want is an extension of the term. Instead of getting it paid back in the next twelve months, we want that term extended another three years.

The lender loses nothing by doing this. He or she gets much of the money now in cash. In three years, the lender gets more back! In the meantime, we've saved our property from foreclosure.

(See also the section on Fannie Mae in the chapter on refinance.)

6. TRY TO SELL THE LENDER ON TAX DEFERRAL

In many cases, when the lender receives the balloon payment from you, he or she is going to have to pay taxes on it. Even though the money you have been paying monthly may have been interest only, chances are that almost all of the balloon payment is principal and as such may be taxable. That means that when you pay, a big chunk is going to go not to the lender, but to Uncle Sam.

What about getting together with the lender and a good tax consultant. Perhaps among the three of you, a plan could be arranged to extend the loan, save the lender from paying big taxes to the government, and save the property from foreclosure. Remember, when the lender doesn't get money all in one big chunk, such as a balloon payment, and instead gets it spread out over a period of years, he or she can defer taxes on it. The tax angle may make the lender want to defer the loan more than you!

7. TAKE IN PARTNERS

If you can't work with the lender, then perhaps it's time to find people who you can work with. Perhaps it's time to take in some partners.

There are many ways for partners to provide benefits to both you and the lender.

You can take in partners to refinance the property. Let's say that you have a second mortgage for 30,000 dollars, all due in a balloon payment. What about if you could find six people each with 5,000 dollars. They could form a partnership, pool their resources, and then loan the amount to you at, say, eighteen percent interest.

The interest rate would be attractive to them, and they would have the property as security.

The money would be used to pay off the existing mortgage with a balloon and to give you a new mortgage that was amortized over, say, ten years.

For the partners there is a steady cash flow for ten years at eighteen percent interest on their money—not a bad deal. For you there are higher payments (because of a surely higher interest rate and amortization), but there's also the fact that the balloon is paid off.

In the above example, if the balloon were for twelve percent payable interest only until paid, your payments would be 300 dollars per month. The same 30,000 dollars amortized over ten years at eighteen percent interest would be 720 dollars per month. The increase to you would be 420 dollars per month. But that's 420 dollars per month as opposed to 30,000 dollars all in one chunk. If interest rates ever do drop and mortgage money ever does become plentiful, you could refinance to a lower interest rate.

You can also make the institutional lender a partner. You owe money to a bank on a balloon payment. You're not going to pay, and they won't refinance. You're going to lose the property, and you don't have enough equity in it to allow you to get very much, if anything, out on a foreclosure sale.

Offer to make the bank a partner. In exchange for refinancing the property (you'll continue to make the payments entirely on your own), you'll give them a percentage of the equity at the time of sale.

In a case like this, start by offering five percent. You can go as high as you need to, as long as it still makes sense for you. If you're going to lose it anyway, fifty percent isn't too high.

You might instead make the private lender a partner. Make the same offer as I just described to the private lender who holds the balloon. Give him or her this option. The lender can extend the mortgage indefinitely and you'll make the same payments with the following provision—when the property is sold, the lender will get a piece of equity. Again, start at five percent and work up to as high as you need to.

8. TRY FOR A REFINANCE

In today's market, it's true, refinance is difficult if not impossible. But if you have an institutional lender who holds the mortgage with the balloon, you have an excellent source of refinancing right at hand. The institutional lender is already set up to handle real estate financing. Go to the lender and try to get him or her to finance. That doesn't mean begging. It means pointing out the advantages of a refinance. These include avoiding the cost and the time spent for a foreclosure, a higher interest rate (which you offer to pay to get the refinance), and continued cash flow from a willing borrower. You have strong arguments—you just have to pursue them.

There's another refinancing alternative that's available to some borrowers. If it turns out that you have another piece of property (other than the one on which the balloon is coming due), you can think about refinancing that other piece. For example, let's say that you own two houses, the one in which you live and a rental house that has a balloon on it. You might consider refinancing your own home (if you can't get a refinance on the rental property) and then using that loan to pay off the balloon.

A couple once came to me with a balloon payment problem on a commercial property. They had a 270,000-dollar balloon payment due on a second trust deed on a building worth 1.2 million dollars. They could not afford to refinance at current market rates and did not have any other source for the money. The solution: A local bank had seven condominiums that it had foreclosed on. We proposed that the couple would buy the seven condominiums if the lender would create a new 370,000-dollar "second." Of that, 270,000 dollars would be used to pay off the current balloon and the additional 100,000 dollars would be used as the down payment on the condominiums. This way the lender solved the couple's problem in return for their solving the bank's problem.

9. LOOK FOR OTHER SOURCES OF CASH

Thus far, I've only suggested going to the holder of the balloon or other institutional lenders. But there are lots of people out there with money, even during a recession. My suggestion is that you do everything possible to find them. Here are some options:

Check in your local paper for people who advertise money to lend on real estate.

Advertise in your local paper under "money wanted".

Check with local real estate brokers and title insurance companies. They often know who has money to lend.

10. GET THE HOLDER OF THE SECOND MORTGAGE TO SUBORDINATE

Subordination simply means that the holder of a junior (second or higher) mortgage agrees to hold that mortgage in a junior position while you go ahead and refinance a first mortgage underneath. It's really a simple concept.

Say you have a home on which you owe a "first" and a "second." The "second" has a balloon coming due. You want to refinance, but no one will lend you money on a "second," and you can't get a big enough "first" to pay off both the existing "first" and the "second."

If the holder of the "second" will subordinate, you can get a new "first" while retaining the "second." The proceeds of the new "first" will pay off the old "first" and some of the existing "second." This way the holder of the "second" gets some of the money (perhaps half or more) paid off in cash and retains a "second" for the balance. This is a good incentive for the holder of the balloon "second" because it avoids foreclosure and gets him or her some cash.

11. GET THE MONEY TO PAY OFF THE BALLOON IN THE FORM OF AN UNSECURED LINE OF CREDIT

Many banks today offer lines of credit to their customers. This is uncollateralized lending, in other words, personal loans. Usually the way these work is that we establish credit with the bank. Then, once our credit is accepted, we get a line of credit. The line can be for anything from 1,000 to 50,000 dollars or more, depending on our credit worthiness and our ability to repay.

Once the credit line is established, to get money we simply let the bank know how much we need and they make the cash available instantly, usually through our checking account.

It is often possible to get many lines of credit. That is, you can go around to different banks and establish lines of credit with each of them.

The whole point here is that if you establish lines of credit with banks *before* you get into foreclosure because of a balloon "second," you probably can get the money you need to pay off that "second" from the lines of credit. (If you wait until after you're in foreclosure, the bank's credit-reporting agency may pick up the recorded notice of default and you may not be able to get a line of credit.)

Once your lines of credit are in place and your balloon comes due (and none of the other alternatives work), you can simply borrow on the lines of credit to pay off the balloon.

The problem here is that often the sources of the lines of credit charge a relatively high interest rate. This can be several percentage points higher than the bank's prime rate. Additionally, they usually require repayment in full in five years or less. That means you could end up with a high payment.

The whole point, however, is to avoid foreclosure, and the line of credit could be viewed as a temporary means to do this. You get a line of credit while you're seeking other more permanent (and less costly) ways of financing the balloon.

12. ANOTHER WAY TO RAISE CASH IS TO EITHER SELL OR BORROW ON OUR PERSONAL PROPERTY

Perhaps we have a boat, a motor home, or something else of value. Finance companies or banks can usually arrange a loan for a percentage of the value of such things. If we really don't want or need them, we might be able to sell through an ad in the paper.

But keep in mind that if we borrow on personal property, we will undoubtedly be paying a high interest rate. Therefore, this procedure (like the one noted in the previous section on unsecured lines of credit) should be viewed as a short-term solution while we raise the money otherwise to cover the balloon.

13. INCREASE AMOUNT OWED ON "SECOND" FOR COMMISSIONS

We can offer to increase the amount we owe to the holder of the balloon mortgage in exchange for extending the payment period. For example, let's say that we owe 25,000 dollars on a second mortgage with a balloon that is coming due in six months. We know the balloon is coming due and so does the holder of the mortgage. We can bet that he or she is nearly as worried about our paying as we are.

We go to see the holder and say we simply can't raise the cash because of both our personal situation and the state of the economy. In today's economy, the holder should have no trouble understanding that.

Now we offer to increase the amount of the "second." We say that instead of owing 25,000 dollars, we'll owe 27,500 dollars. In exchange for this, we want an extension on the time we have to pay. We can start by asking for a two-year extension, which might get whittled back to one year.

If the "second" holder doesn't have a pressing need for the money, he or she might very well accept our offer.

14. OFFER A HIGHER INTEREST RATE

This is essentially the same as the last way, except that instead of offering the holder of the "second" a bigger mortgage, we offer a higher interest rate. Instead of the twelve percent we've been paying, we offer fourteen percent in exchange for at least a year's extension on the balloon.

15. CONSIDER GIVING THE PROPERTY BACK

This is the same thing as a deed in lieu of foreclosure. If it appears that you simply aren't going to be able to raise the money, and if it is clear that the mortgage holder is going to pursue foreclosure right to a sale, then offer to give the holder a deed to the property. Perhaps this can have a price tag attached. Maybe you'll give the holder a deed in exchange for letting you keep the property for a year rent free, or maybe you'll give the holder a deed for 3,000 dollars in cash.

The whole point is that *if you're going to lose the property any-*

way, by giving a deed in lieu of foreclosure you at least save your credit.

16. GET THE BALLOON DISCOUNTED

This works with planning ahead. A second mortgage is rarely worth its face value in cash. For example, a "second" with a year to run for 10,000 dollars might only be worth 7,000 dollars in cash today. If we're planning ahead and we know we have a balloon to pay, wouldn't it be better to pay 7,000 dollars today than 10,000 dollars a year from now?

Talk to the lender who has the balloon. See what his or her motivation is. See if the lender is willing to sell that "second" at discount, then try to raise the cash. It saves money in the long run.

17. USE A BALLOON TO PURCHASE

This technique involves real planning ahead. It involves planning *before* you buy the property.

When it's time to purchase the property, offer the seller a short-term mortgage (say six months) with a balloon on it. To a seller, this is almost like cash. It is saying that the seller will get the money, but he or she will just have to wait six months. Most sellers regard this offer as good as gold.

But, as a condition for purchase, insist that the seller reduce the price substantially.

If the seller goes for this, once you have the property you should be able to refinance for enough to pay off the seller's mortgage. In effect, you didn't pull any money out of your pocket to influence the seller to reduce the price, but you used the temptation of a balloon to accomplish it.

These are just some of the methods that can be used to overcome the problem of a balloon payment coming due. But we shouldn't think these are the *only* methods. The only real limitation is our own creativity. Remember the story of the Arab and the seventeen camels. We've just had seventeen different solutions to a balloon. If none of them work for you, try to be like the wise man. Come up with the eighteenth camel (solution) that will work!

Chapter Ten
IS HOMESTEADING AN OPTION?

"I cannot give you a formula for success, but I can give you the formula for failure—which is: Try to please everybody."

—Herbert Bayard Swope

Most people have heard about homesteading. We remember it as part of the Oklahoma land rush of the 1800s and as part of the way our western states were won. Pioneers staked out or homesteaded a plot of land, and it became theirs.

Homesteading has continued on into the present (although the form is now somewhat different), and many people believe that it presents a viable option to foreclosure today. "My house is my castle, and as long as I remain in it no one can move me out" is the sentiment, and the legal counterpart is homesteading.

Is homesteading a real option in today's world, or is it just a relic from the past that promises but does not deliver?

THE TRACK RECORD

Formal homesteading came about in many states during the Great Depression of the 1930s. At that time people were losing all they owned, including their homes. To stop this some states passed homestead laws that said, in effect, a person could not be forced out of his or her house for having not paid the creditors.

It sounds like a lot of protection, and given the values enacted in the 1930s, it was. But today we have a different world. Today homesteading not only offers limited protections, but it often can also work *against* a person facing foreclosure!

HOW IT WORKS

Homesteading works in this manner: A homeowner (it usually has to be your home, not some investment property) at some point decides that he or she needs to homestead the property. In states where homestead laws exist, the owner now secures and fills out a special homesteading form (each state has its own form requirements, and the form and information on your state's homestead laws may be obtained from nearly any title insurance or escrow company, real estate broker, or attorney.)

Once the form is filled out, the homeowner records it at the county recorder's office. (In some areas publishing may also be required.)

That's it.

PROTECTIONS

Once the homestead declaration is on file, it generally protects by prohibiting creditors from forcing a house to be sold at auction to satisfy debts.

LIMITS

The amount of protection, however, is usually small. Remember, these laws came out of the 1930s when money was worth much more than it is today. Even with increases in recent years the dollar limits tend to remain low. In California, for example, the limits might be 30,000 dollars for a single person and 45,000 dollars for a head of a household.

This is the maximum protection offered. What's important to understand is that this amount refers to your *equity* in your property. If you own a house worth 100,000 dollars but have only 10,000 dollars in equity, then your protection is limited to the 10,000 dollars. Remember, only your equity is protected under the homestead law.

This means, for example, that if your home is worth 100,000 dollars, you owe 25,000 dollars, and your equity is 75,000 dollars, you would still have 45,000 dollars unprotected as a single person in California (30,000 dollars as a head of a household). Creditors could still force a sale to recoup the amount *over* the homestead limit.

CALCULATING HOMESTEAD PROTECTION

value of property	$100,000
mortgage	−25,000
equity	$75,000
maximum homestead	−45,000
amount not protected	$30,000

Second, homesteading normally *does not afford protection against mortgages placed on the property* prior *to the homestead declaration.*

Consider this carefully. We have a mortgage on our property. Suddenly, because of external reasons, we can't make the payments, so we look to homesteading as a way to save our home.

Wrong! We gain no protection if the mortgage was placed on the property *prior* to the time we filed the homestead declaration. (In some areas we gain no protection if the mortgage is placed on the property even *after* we file the declaration.)

PROTECTIONS

If that's the case, then what good is the homesteading?

The answer is it protects us against liens and judgments placed against our home *after* it has been filed. Let's take an example.

A lien is anything involving money that ties up our property. For example, we hire a builder to construct a patio in our backyard. The builder has costs of material such as cement, lumber, and steel and costs of labor.

We agree to pay the builder when he or she is done. But suddenly we get ill, lose our job, and have no money to pay.

Of course, the builder isn't concerned about our plight. He or she did the job and wants the money. If we don't pay, the builder can slap a mechanic's lien against our property. This lien ties up our property and with court action, could actually force a sale in order to get the money with which to pay off the builder.

If, however, as soon as we discover the costs of our illness and our other financial problems we file a declaration of homestead, *before* the mechanic's lien is filed, we are protected up to the amounts specified by our state.

Let's consider another example. Jody is a spendthrift. She has credit cards and is constantly charging items. When the bills come due, she borrows on other credit cards to make the minimum payment.

Jody is irresponsible, but she's not stupid. She has equity in a house, and one day, when she discovers she has used up all her credit, she realizes the banks will be coming after her—and her house. So she immediately files a declaration of homestead on her home.

When she can't make the minimum payments on the charge cards, the lenders take action. Eventually they go to court and get a judgment against Jody for the money she owes. They seek to force the sale of her home to collect. Because she homesteaded *before* the judgment on her house was issued, however, they are stopped up to the limits in Jody's state.

PROBLEMS WITH HOMESTEADING

The advantages of homesteading should be obvious from the two previous examples. The disadvantages, however, are not quite so clear but are nevertheless very real.

All institutional and most private lenders know about homesteading and the difficulties it can cause them. The last thing they want is to be caught by a declaration of homestead. Therefore they usually pay a few dollars per month to a service that keeps track of all homesteads recorded in their county.

The minute a homestead is recorded, the lenders are notified, and they immediately check their computers to see if the person has credit or has been offered credit by them. If the homesteader is indeed a borrower or a potential borrower, that person's credit rating immediately crashes to zero. No intelligent lender will loan a dime to a person who has homesteaded a house.

It's like waving a red flag. If you ever want to see your credit dry up overnight, just try homesteading your house.

Therein, of course, lies the danger. By homesteading, we might lose the opportunity to obtain the very credit that might see us through and out of our current financial difficulties.

Homesteading, therefore, is a double-edged sword. We have to balance the risks of losing credit with the hoped-for benefits of saving our house.

(Note: It is possible to record an abandonment of homestead, thereby removing the protection from the records. This, however, does not usually offer immediate help to our credit. Just notifying a lender that a homestead has been abandoned isn't going to make things all good again. The lender will remain suspicious about why the homestead was recorded in the first place, and it might still be a long time before we can get credit.)

THE BOTTOM LINE

All of this is to say that homesteading is not really a useful device to protect us from foreclosure of our mortgage. It does offer some protections to our home from other creditors, with the drawbacks I just outlined.

DON'T MAKE THE HOMESTEAD DECISION UNAIDED!

If you are considering homesteading your property, first see a good attorney. Have the laws in your state explained fully so that you understand both the benefits and the risks. Acting rashly with homesteading could throw you out of the frying pan into the fire.

Chapter Eleven
SOURCES OF CASH YOU MIGHT NOT HAVE CONSIDERED

"If a man is wise, he gets rich. An' if he gets rich, he gets foolish, or his wife does. That's what keeps the money moving around."

—Finley Peter Dunne

The best, the easiest, and the most obvious way to stop foreclosure is to pay the money due. Pay the monthly payments or pay the balloon payments. (It works every time.) The mortgage can't go into foreclosure until we default or don't pay. If we pay, we don't default—ergo no foreclosure.

Of course, that's the whole problem—raising the money. Sometimes we overlook opportunities, however, by not thinking creatively. We tend to look for the obvious and not for the subtle. For example, consider this story:

Two female ostriches were running along the sand in Australia. Now I'm sure that every reader knows the thing that ostriches are remarkable for. When they are in danger, they stick their heads in the sand. These two female ostriches were no different.

They were running along when suddenly one of them turned and there were two male ostriches in the distance running toward them. "Watch out for the boys," the ostrich squeaked to her companion, and they took off at top speed.

A few minutes later, the second ostrich turned and saw that the boys were closing fast. "They're gaining on us," she said to her companion. "What shall we do?"

The first ostrich replied, "Let's stick our heads in the sand."

"That's a good idea," the second answered, and they both did.

Now you have to picture this in your mind. There are the two female ostriches bent way over, their backs to the boys, with their heads in the sand.

Just at this time, one of the male ostriches turns to the other—and can you guess what he said?

The male ostrich turned to his friend and said, "Hey, where'd the girls go?"

This little story helps point out the fact that things are not always what they seem. We can think we see the goal and the way things are going so clearly and then, out of the blue, there's a sudden change that turns around our whole way of thinking. That's the way it is in foreclosure and in particular in raising money to stop foreclosure.

In this chapter, I'm going to give you different ideas that you might or might not be able to use to raise cash to stop foreclosure. Some we've already mentioned, others are new, and yet others may seem totally farfetched. But remember, what might seem farfetched to one reader might be just the answer to another.

Study these suggestions. (By the way, you might be able to come up with some better ones yourself.) Maybe one of them, upon consideration, will seem a lot better than it first appears. Maybe it will give you a whole new perspective that will enable you to avoid foreclosure.

INCOME ADDERS

WAGE OR BONUS ADVANCE

Have you been working for your employer for a long time? Does your employer value your services? Would he or she be concerned about your effectiveness at work if you were worried about losing your house to foreclosure?

If you have a decent employer, yes indeed he or she would be worried. You can be darn sure that once you get into foreclosure your employer is going to be wondering just what kind of an employee gets into such trouble.

On the other hand, if we plan ahead and then see our employer *before* we get into foreclosure, it could be a different story. Our employer might think, "This person's got good management skill and is conscientious. He or she is looking ahead and trying to plan for it. That makes this person even more valuable."

Asking your employer for a handout undoubtedly won't work. But what about if you have vacation time coming? What about a bonus due at the end of the year? What about a portion of next year's wages?

If your employer knows you, trusts you, finds you valuable, and is able, he or she might act to help you out.

BORROW ON INCOME TAX REFUND

If you have a salary that has withholding, chances are you might be due for a sizable income tax return, particularly if you didn't have your withholding reduced (for example, by claiming fewer dependents) when the new tax law went into effect. A few hundred to a thousand dollars or more might be coming your way after you file, and that could be enough to allow you to catch up a payment or two on your mortgage, thereby avoiding foreclosure. You can borrow now on next year's tax refund.

Another method of generating money from income taxes is to increase your number of withholding allowances to increase your monthly income. By law, you can now claim up to fourteen exemptions without your employer having to go to the I.R.S. for approval. The previous limit was only nine. This works if it turns out that because of the big mortgage on your house, you'll have a big interest deduction on your taxes when they are calculated. Rather than wait until the end of the year and then get a big return, you can get the money each month during the year by increasing withholding allowances and decreasing withholding.

Warning: Don't use this method unless you've consulted with your attorney, accountant, or financial consultant, and he or she advises you to. My personal feeling is it could be far less worse to lose your house than to decrease your withholding and then later discover you had made a mistake and owed the government money at twenty percent interest.

CREDIT UNION

A credit union is another good source of cash. Often we belong to a credit union through our place of employment or through our union. Some people have credit union membership through former employment. Regardless, if we do have membership in a credit union, it can be an excellent source of cash for us to cure mortgage problems with.

Credit unions often will make loans directly on property. Those that won't will make personal loans to us.

There are usually two benefits with credit union loans. The first is that because we're a member, we can usually get more favorable treatment. Second, the credit union has payroll deductions. Typically, interest rates are lower than at many commercial finance companies and can be somewhat better than the best bank loans because they are nonprofit. But the credit unions are in business to stay solvent, so they won't lend us money at a rate less than they can borrow it at.

The problem is that very frequently credit union loans are for relatively small amounts of money. Uncollateralized loans might be for just a few thousand at maximum. On property, however, the unions might be able to loan the money you need.

I used to think that since I had my own company, I did not qualify to join any credit unions. But I found out it was like joining one of those membership stores. My wife heard XYZ Store had the lowest prices in town and wanted me to see if I could finagle a membership in some way. I went to see them and they said that I had to be a government employee, or be related to a government employee, or have known a government employee, or—I think you get the idea. I then found out I could join many credit unions.

Think of the credit union as a friend that will help you out if it can. Go see, and find out what it can do for you. Unless you explore every possible source, you'll never know.

FRIENDS AND RELATIVES

Then there's the old standby, friends and relatives. Do not be too proud to ask a friend or a relative for a loan to save your house.

If you are, you probably won't save your house. Ask any people you know well what you could do for them to motivate them to help you out of your dilemma.

In today's economy, friends and relatives regularly help buyers make down payments. Many parents lend or give children the money for a down payment. Friends will often lend money at good interest rates secured by a note on property to someone they know well.

Don't overlook this possibility. If a friend or a relative might lend money to help you buy the property, he or she might also lend you money now to help you stop foreclosure.

A word of warning here: Don't try to minimize your problem. People respect a person who is candid, even if they don't like what he or she says. Spell out what you need the money for. Show what the problem is, whether it is past due payments or a balloon, and then very carefully present your plan for catching up and show how the present borrowing or gift you hope to get fits in. When you borrow from friends or relatives, make it a businesslike thing. Every lender —*everyone*—likes to see how you are going to spend the money and how he or she will eventually get repaid (in whatever form).

SWEAT EQUITY
Sweat equity usually comes into play when it's time to purchase a house. Instead of providing a down payment in cash, the buyer buys a run-down piece of property at a far lower price and then personally works to fix it up. The buyer's sweat from labor is what builds the equity.

There are two ways to use sweat equity when we are faced with foreclosure. The first comes into play if we see that we have less than fifteen percent in equity in our present home. We then allow it to go, trying to give a deed in lieu of foreclosure at the last minute to avoid credit problems.

At the same time, we buy a "fixer-upper." This is a run-down house that needs sweat to fix it up. We get out of our old situation into a new one where we can use our own work to build up our interest in the property. Instead of having to come up with a large down payment, we buy for little or no down.

A second way to use sweat equity is to secure a home improvement loan on our present house before we get too deeply into foreclosure. Usually we don't get this money until we complete certain portions of the work. Instead of hiring a contractor to do the work, we do it ourselves. Instead of paying a contractor for the work done, we pay ourselves with the money loaned from the bank. We then use that money to pay off a balloon or to fix a mortgage in debt.

(The way a true home improvement loan works as opposed to other types of loans is that the work must be done to get the loan money. The reason is that the loan amount is based not on the present value of the property, but on the value at the time the repair work is complete.)

UNSECURED BANK LOANS

This is an uncollateralized loan. In this kind of loan, we basically pledge ourselves as security. We guarantee to repay the loan without putting up any specific piece of property, real or personal.

To get an unsecured bank loan, we usually have to have sterling credit and no need for the money. A bank lender will chase us around the block to give us money, providing we can prove we have no real need for it. But let us show that we need it to bail out a mortgage and we might as well be talking to a stone wall. Once again, it's a matter of planning ahead. If we want to get an unsecured bank loan, we had better count on doing it long before we actually need the money.

PERSONAL PROPERTY LOAN

Many finance companies are willing to make loans secured by personal property or a combination of personal and real property. In a personal property loan, we pledge not our real estate or just our good credit, but our personal property. This might be in a variety of forms from a car to furniture, to a refrigerator, to anything else. (In the general scheme of things, real property refers to land and things built on it—in other words, real estate. Everything else is personal property.)

The problem with personal property loans is that very often the interest rate is extremely high.

PASSBOOK LOANS

If we have a balloon coming due *and* if we have the money to pay for it in the bank, *but* we don't want to take the money out, there is an alternative. Any bank will arrange a passbook loan. This is a loan we make using the money in our savings account as collateral.

Since the collateral is savings and since the bank is paying us interest on the savings, the charge for the loan here is usually very low, rarely over two percent above the savings account rate. This can be a real advantage.

Consider: If we borrow on the property, we might end up with a mortgage at fifteen percent. On the other hand, we might have our money in a savings and loan, earning ten percent in a long-term account. We might be able to borrow against this at eleven percent. Now we still have our money in the account (although we might be able to withdraw until the loan is paid back), we have the cash to save the property, and we have it an interest rate of four percent below market.

COMORTGAGOR

What do we do if we didn't plan ahead? It's all well and good to say plan ahead when there's time to plan ahead. But what if we've already gotten into default, a sale is pending, and we need the money? We want a bank loan to bail us out, but it's too late to plan ahead. What do we do?

The answer here is that we arrange for a comortgagor. This can be anyone who is willing to vouch for the mortgage along with us. Usually it's a relative or a very close friend who trusts us personally and our ability to get the money back.

It's a toss-up as to whether or not a bank will accept a comortgagor. Some will and some won't. But don't listen to a lender who says it's never done. It's done all the time. You just have to find a bank who's policy is such that it will accept a comortgagor.

The comortgagor signs along with us and becomes *personally* responsible for the repayment of the debt. If the person has good credit and assets, the bank should be more than willing to go along. Since that person is vouching for our debt, we will have to find a really good friend or relative who is willing to go along with us here.

ASSIGNING THE IMPOUND ACCOUNT

Many mortgages have impound accounts. These are separate accounts into which we pay each month for the purpose of paying property taxes and property insurance. Often over a period of years, the amount of money in the impound account builds up to the point where we have an excess there. The excess could be a few dollars, a few hundred, or in some cases, even a few thousand. In theory, the mortgage company is supposed to pay this money back to us when the excess appears, but sometimes that doesn't happen.

If we have extra money in our impound account, we should be able to have that money assigned to our lender to help pay off back payments. For the lender, it's an easy task to get to that money. It's simply switching from one account the lender is holding to another.

LIQUIDATING ASSETS

Other Property "Seconds"
Given the real estate merry-go-round that we've had for the last few years, there are lots of us who have sold homes and in order to sell had to take back paper. Usually this is in the form of a second mortgage. Maybe we are receiving some money each month in payment on this "second."

This mortgage can be a ready source of cash. Second mortgages can be sold for cash. We can find someone who wants that "second" and convert it into what we need—hard currency.

Of course, there's a drawback. Selling paper mortgages almost always involves a discount. Cash is worth more than paper, and so we have to discount the mortgage to find its cash value.

The amount of discount will vary, depending on the difference between the interest rate we're charging and the going mortgage rate, the length before the mortgage is due, how well the borrowers have been paying, and the chances for collecting in today's market. Discounts from ten to fifty percent are common.

"That's a big discount." I can already hear the shouting.

Yes it is, but as in most things in life, there's a trade-off. Is it worth the discount to save your house? Only you can make the decision.

(Investors who will buy "seconds" advertise regularly in the papers. Brokers, escrow companies, title companies, accountants, and lawyers are also good sources to direct you to such investors.)

Other Property
Some of us own more than one piece of property. Perhaps there's that little lot out by the lake or up in the hills that we bought ten years ago and on which we are counting on building on some day. We bought it years ago, but it's in the back of our minds and we have all but forgotten about it.

116

"Oh, but we can't touch that. It's our dream!"

Maybe it is, but what good is a dream in the future if we're living in a nightmare today? Maybe that lot could be sold to someone else and we could use the money to cover a balloon or fix the owed payments on our home. Maybe we could convert that future dream for getting us awake and moving today. (Besides, we can always go back and buy back our lot or another one after a while, when we are better off financially than right now.)

Refinance Other Property

What about not selling other property we have, but refinancing it? In the case of a lot such as just mentioned, this could be a problem. Financing bare land is very difficult. But what if we own another house, an apartment building, or any other piece of real estate? What about going to a lender and taking out a mortgage on that other piece of property, and then using the proceeds to solve our problem on our current property?

Some people have the feeling that this shouldn't be done. They believe that each property should carry its own weight. They somehow think that it's breaking the rules of the game if we borrow on the property on Green Street to pay off the mortgage on the property on Blue Street.

This is fallacious thinking. The best way of looking at it is to say, "I own property. It is divided into one, two, or five (or however many) parcels. What I own is the property, not simply the parcels."

To put it another way, if we have a bad infection on our arm, would we refuse to take medicine through our mouth because it wasn't our mouth that was infected?

We do whatever we have to to save our property from foreclosure. If that means borrowing on another piece, that's perfectly all right.

The Blanket Mortgage

Along these lines, there's another technique that sometimes works. Instead of borrowing on one piece to pay off the mortgage on another, how about getting a single mortgage that covers both pieces?

A mortgage that covers more than one piece of property is called a blanket mortgage.

A blanket mortgage is sometimes far easier to get than a mortgage on any single parcel. The reason is that the lender feels more secure with a blanket. He or she feels that there is a lot of security. If we don't make the payments, then there are several pieces of property that can be held accountable.

For us, a blanket mortgage is probably a less desirable risk than others. Instead of risking only one parcel, we are now risking many. On the other hand, without the blanket mortgage, we might simply not be able to raise money. If it's a choice between not getting the money we need to cure a mortgage and getting it, most people I know would choose the blanket.

Life Insurance

If we have a life insurance policy, we have some cash value in it. Whole life policies typically build up equity over the years. If we've been paying year after year, we might have enough money stored in our life insurance policy to save ourselves from foreclosure.

The procedure here is to contact our insurance agent and our insurance company and ask them what our cash value is.

Some people don't want to surrender their insurance policies for the cash. In those cases, it might be possible to borrow against the policy. Usually the interest rate is a little bit more than the difference between what the insurance policy pays and the current market interest rate.

TEMPORARY EMPLOYMENT OF OUR SPOUSE

If our spouse isn't working, then one good source of generating a steady stream of cash is for him or her to get a job. In perhaps fifty percent of American families, at least one spouse isn't working. In those families, it is often a matter of putting tradition aside in favor of necessity. Yes, it may seem that in our mother and father's time, only one spouse worked. But today, with today's economic problems, survival may dictate both getting jobs, at least long enough to get over the current financial bind. (If neither is working, we should consider temporary employment for either one or both spouses; if we are single and not working, we could obtain temporary employment.)

OTHER SOURCES

There are other sources of cash that we haven't even touched upon.

These include borrowing against a pension fund (such borrowing might not always be possible) and assigning the proceeds of a lawsuit or other sources of revenue coming to us in the future.

Something as simple as getting a cash advance on credit cards might work. Today for people with even modest credit it is possible to get hundreds or even thousands of separate Visa or Mastercard cards, each from a different lending institution and each with a separate credit limit. We could borrow tens of thousands of dollars this way.

(*Caution:* Such borrowing is *not advised* unless you have a specific payback plan. It costs to borrow in terms of high interest rates. The money unwisely borrowed on credit cards today could come back tomorrow in the form of enormous bills, ruined credit, bankruptcy—and foreclosure.)

As I mentioned earlier, these suggestions are not written in stone. Some of them might not apply. Others might seem to be only distant possibilities. But there might be a few that ring a bell.

Don't be like the ostriches. Don't think only one way. Just because you don't see a solution doesn't mean it isn't out there. The problem could be just that you're hiding your head in the sand.

Chapter Twelve

THE SOLDIERS' AND SAILORS' CIVIL RELIEF ACT

"It's not over until it's over!"
—Yogi Berra

Let's consider the incredible story of a friend of mine, Harry.

Harry is in his early twenties. Back in 1980 when real estate was still booming, he decided he wanted to buy a home. With the help of a broker, he obtained a large loan from a savings and loan association and bought a home. Of course the interest rate and the monthly payments were sky-high, but Harry figured he'd soon sell for a profit.

A year later Harry decided to join the Navy. He rented out the house but found he couldn't rent it for anything like the payments. Very soon it became evident that he was going to lose the property. The savings and loan was going to foreclose and because Harry was in the service 1,500 miles away, there appeared to be little he could do.

Then he contacted a Navy attorney, who brought to his attention the Soldiers' and Sailors' Civil Relief Act.

This act was passed years ago to help people just like Harry. It offers him protection against foreclosure in his situation.

Harry was amazed to discover that it temporarily suspends all but judicial foreclosure. The savings and loan could not foreclose out of court on his mortgage once he informed it he was in the service and intended seeking relief under the Soldiers' and Sailors' Civil Relief Act.

To foreclose, the savings and loan would have to go to court. Even there, it was uncertain that it would prevail.

Certainly Harry was delighted with this turn of events. He was protected for as long as he qualified and was in the service.

SPECIAL BONUS INTEREST REDUCTION

But what really turned Harry's head around was when he learned another provision of the act. Harry had been paying fifteen percent interest on his mortgage. Now, while he was in the service, *the interest rate on the mortgage was automatically reduced to six percent!*

Yes, you read that correctly. The maximum rate allowed under the act is six percent. (Remember, when this act became law, six percent was considered a high interest rate, and it has not been changed since.)

HOW OTHERS BENEFIT

I'm sure we're all thinking that this was great for Harry—but how does that affect us? Going into the service to avoid foreclosure is a pretty drastic solution. Some people might even say that the solution is worse than the problem!

Certainly I'm not suggesting that you go into the service if you have a foreclosure problem. (If, however, you are going into the service, this might provide a solution. Just remember that the mortgage has to have been put on your house *prior* to your going in.)

What I have seen, in doing research for this book, however, are a number of shrewd borrowers who have used this to gain protection for themselves. Here is what they did.

When it became apparent that these borrowers were facing foreclosure, they went out and found themselves a person in or going into the military. It might have been a friend or a relative or just someone they met. They then transferred *a portion* of their property to this individual.

Now this person in the service owns a home. That home is being threatened with foreclosure. So the person in the service sends a registered letter to the savings and loan notifying it that he or she is in the armed services and is seeking protection under the Soldiers' and Sailors' Civil Relief Act.

Does it work?

In the cases I saw, the savings and loan was intimidated. The penalties for going through with a foreclosure when the act has been invoked are strict. The savings and loan began investigating. In my research, every savings and loan in this situation did one of three things:

    1. They begged to negotiate new terms.

    2. They began judicial foreclosure, which in most cases took three or four times longer than out-of-court foreclosure on a trust deed.

    3. They agreed to the six percent interest rate and a delay while the owner was in the service!

THE BOTTOM LINE

Of course, this is basically a holding action. It is designed to get the lender to back off for a while or to renegotiate the mortgage. It's not likely to have any permanent effect on the mortgage situation.

If you're desperately seeking to avoid foreclosure, it might act like a Band-aid. What you should do is seek the advice of an attorney who is familiar with the Soldiers' and Sailors' Civil Relief Act *and* your own personal situation and property. Don't act rashly. Find out if in your own particular case this makes sense. (It may not.)

Remember, *for this to be effective you must send the lender a legal copy of the deed showing that title has been transferred to someone in the service and the name of that person.*

If this act is of interest to you, I'm sure you have additional questions about procedure, qualifications, and so on. In my research I discovered that the act was specifically written in layman's language so that the average soldier or sailor could understand it.

Therefore to aid you I'm enclosing a copy of a governmental pamphlet explaining the act.

CONGRESSIONAL PAMPHLET

INTRODUCTION

You may have been ordered to report for active duty with the armed forces. You may owe money on your car, your home and perhaps even on a personal loan. At the time you made these debts you may have been earning considerably more than you will earn as a servicemember. Once in the service, your military pay may not be enough to provide for all these debts.

Congress realized that many servicemembers would, from time to time, be confronted with this problem. Therefore it decided to give you some protection in the interest of national defense. This protection is found in the Soldiers' and Sailors' Civil Relief Act, which, as the name suggests, affords relief with respect to various civil and personal obligations but does not cover criminal offenses. The Act is one of a series of Federal laws concerning military service that may be found in the appendix to volume 50 of the United States Code. 50 App. U.S.C. §§ 501-590. The Act is still in effect and, though entitled "Soldiers' and Sailors' Civil Relief Act," protects others including members of the Air Force, Marine Corps and Coast Guard. 50 App. U.S.C. §§ 464, 466(c) and 511.

The Act does not, repeat does not, wipe out any of your obligations. Rather, it temporarily suspends the right of your creditors to use a court to compel you to pay if, but only if, the court finds that your inability to pay is due to your military service. Your obligation to honor your debts still exists, and after your release from active duty you will then have to pay them. In short, the idea behind the Civil Relief Act is to suspend, in certain cases, court proceedings during your tour of duty in the military service so that upon your return to civilian life you might have an opportunity to be heard and to take measures to protect your interests.

CAUTION: *This Act is highly technical. Remember, your benefits under it are limited. Do not assume that you know all the details of the Act after reading this pamphlet. It is intended only to give you a simplified summary so that you will have some idea of the protections the Act affords. If, after reading this pamphlet, you believe some provisions of the Act may be of immediate benefit to you, you should discuss their application to your problem with your civilian attorney or with a legal assistance officer of the armed forces. If you desire the services of a legal assistance officer, go to the nearest military installation and ask for his help.*

How a Lawsuit is Processed

Before discussing the actual provisions of the Act, it might be helpful for you to understand how lawsuits are generally conducted.

The person who brings the suit is known as the "plaintiff." The person against whom the suit is brought is known as the "defendant." The typical lawsuit is begun when the plaintiff, either himself or through an attorney, files a written document called a "complaint" with the proper court. In the complaint he states why he has started the suit. After the complaint is filed, the plaintiff must give the defendant notice that the suit has been started. This is accomplished by means of a "summons." A summons is a formal written notice to the defendant to the effect that a suit has been filed against him and that unless he contests the suit, "judgment" may be entered against him.

If the defendant desires to contest the suit, he will normally file a written document called an "answer" stating why the plaintiff should not win. After a trial at which both sides may be heard, the court enters a judgment in favor of one of the parties. For example, in a lawsuit involving money the judgment may either order the defendant to pay or may state that he owes nothing. If the defendant is ordered to pay, he should remember that, although he does not have any property or money at that time, the judgment may be collected years later.

If the defendant does not file an answer within the time specified in the summons, he is said to have "defaulted." When the defendant has defaulted, the court may enter a "judgment by default" in favor of the plaintiff.

PART I.—GENERAL PROVISIONS

SECTION A. *Who Is Protected*

The Civil Relief Act normally applies only to "persons in the military service." "Persons in the military service" include:

(1) All persons on extended active duty, whether inductees, regulars, members of the National Guard, Reserves, or volunteers, serving with the Army, Navy, Air Force, Marine Corps or Coast Guard;

(2) all officers of the Public Health Service detailed for duty with the military services;

(3) all persons who are training or studying under the supervision of the United States preliminary to induction into military service;

(4) all former citizens of the United States who serve with the Armed Forces of our allies during wartime; and

(5) all persons who have been ordered to report for induction.

In some instances, however, certain benefits are provided for dependents of persons in the military service and for those persons who have guaranteed obligations of service personnel.

SECTION B. *When Are You Protected*

You are protected during the period of your active military duty and, in most instances, for short periods after separation. Active duty begins on the date you enter the service and ends on the date you are separated. Enlisted reservists and draftees have an additional benefit under the Act in that they may ask for relief as soon as they receive orders to report for active duty.

SECTION C. *Where Do You Get the Protection*

The protection of the Civil Relief Act applies to all lawsuits in any court in the United States, from a Justice of the Peace Court to the United States Supreme Court.

PART II.—GENERAL RELIEF PROVISIONS APPLICABLE TO ALL LAWSUITS

SECTION A. *Protection Against Default Judgment*

1. *General.* As has been previously mentioned, a lawsuit begins when the plaintiff files his complaint. If you, the defendant, do not file an answer to the plaintiff's complaint within a certain time after you have received notice of the complaint, the court may then enter its judgment against you. This judgment is known as a "default judgment." However, one of the major benefits that you as a servicemenber on active duty derive from the Civil Relief Act is that a court may not enter a default judgment against you unless a certain definite procedure is followed. How this is done is explained below.

2. *Requiring Military Affidavit.* Under the Act, before a court can enter a default judgment against you, the plaintiff must make

125

and file a statement under oath that you are not in the military service. If he is unable to make such a statement, then he must file a sworn statement (1) that you are in the military service, or (2) that he is unable to find out whether or not you are in the military service.

3. *Rights of the Defendant in the Service.* If the plaintiff files a sworn statement stating you are not in the military service, a default judgment may then be entered against you. If the plaintiff's statement fails to state you are not in the military service, a default judgment may be entered by the court only after it has appointed an attorney to represent you and the attorney is heard in your behalf. An attorney so appointed to represent you has no power to waive any of your rights or bind you by his acts.

Further, in the event the court enters a default judgment, it can require the plaintiff to put up a security deposit. This security will protect you in the event the judgment is later set aside, that is, the security will be used, if necessary, to pay you for any damages you may have suffered as a result of a judgment that was incorrectly entered against you.

4. *False Affidavit.* As noted above, the plaintiff must file a sworn statement concerning your military status. Suppose he swears in that statement that you are not in the military service, knowing that you are—then what? The Act makes such false swearing a crime and the guilty party can be sent to prison for as long as a year, fined not more than $1,000, or both.

5. *Setting Aside a Default Judgment.* If a default judgment is entered against you during your military service, or even thirty days thereafter, you may still have some protection. You may ask the court to reopen the case and to set aside the default judgment. The court will probably do so if you can show:

(1) that your application to open the case is being made within ninety days after your discharge from the service;

(2) that you were harmed or prejudiced by reason of your military service in presenting your side of the case to the court; and

(3) you have a valid, legal defense to the suit.

Even though the plaintiff has been found guilty of false swearing as discussed in previous paragraphs, you must still satisfy all three of these requirements before your case may be reopened.

CAUTION: If you hear, either indirectly through a friend or directly through receipt of a summons, that a lawsuit has been filed against you, don't panic. Instead, see your civilian attorney or legal assistance officer. Let him advise you before you take any action. By acting without such advice you may waive the protection the Act gives you.

It should be noted that your protection against default judgments, as discussed above, applies only when you fail to make "any appearance" in the lawsuit. What acts on your part constitute "any appearance" are too numerous to mention. Furthermore, an act that may not be considered "any appearance" in one court may be in another.

Therefore, you should always get the advice of an attorney. It may be to your advantage for the lawsuit to be tried immediately. But this decision should be made only after an attorney has reviewed the facts of your individual case.

SECTION B. *Stays*

1. *General.* As you have seen, the Act provides some relief from default judgments. This relief is available regardless of what the plaintiff has asked the court to do—be it to allow the plaintiff to adopt your child, to grant a divorce, to award damages for injuries, etc. Because such relief applies generally to all lawsuits, those sections of the Act are referred to as the "general relief" provisions. There are still other important "general relief" provisions in the Act. One of the more important is that which provides for stays of the judicial process. A *stay* is an order of the court stopping or delaying proceedings in the lawsuit until a later date.

2. *How Military Service Affects Stays.* At any stage of a lawsuit you, a servicemember, may ask the court to stay the proceedings. This is true whether you are the plaintiff or the defendant. In addition, the court itself may order the proceedings delayed without being asked. If the court is not asked for a postponement by the person in the military service, then it is not required by the Act to grant one. On the other hand, when a stay is requested by a servicemember, the Act requires the court to grant it unless, in the opinion of the court, the servicemember's ability to prosecute or defend the lawsuit is "not materially affected by reason of his military service."

When you ask for a stay initially, you need only show the court that you are in the service. If the other party to the lawsuit does not want it delayed, he must prove to the court that your military service does not materially affect your ability to prosecute or defend. You have no automatic right to a stay; the judge of the court will decide whether you should have one. If he does grant one, he may order it for the duration of your military service plus three months or he may limit the stay for a shorter period.

However, it should be added that a request for a stay may be "any appearance" for the purposes of a default judgment mentioned above.

SECTION C. *Statutes of Limitations*

In most instances a person who has a right to bring a lawsuit in a court or a proceeding before an administrative board or agency must do so within a certain time limit. The laws and regulations setting this time limit are known as "Statutes of Limitations." These statutes start "running" from the instant the suit or proceeding could first have been filed. A statute of limitations is said to have "run" when the time limit for filing has passed.

Under the "general relief provision" of the Civil Relief Act, these statutes stop "running" while you are in the military service. In order to determine whether a particular statute of limitations has "run," exclude the period of time that you were in the military service.

For example, someone damaged your car in Maryland on January 2, 1961. You entered the service on February 1, 1961, and remain in the service until January 31, 1963. Suppose Maryland's statute of limitation requires suit for damages to be filed with the proper court within three years from the date of the accident. Under the Act the two years you are in the military service will not be counted in the three years you have to file suit. Thus, you will have until January 1, 1966, to file suit.

Suppose in the above example that you had damaged someone else's car. In this instance the other party would also have until January 1, 1966, to bring suit against you.

In both the above examples the accident occurred *before* you entered the service. Nevertheless, the same results would be reached if it had occurred *after* you had entered the service.

PART III.—SPECIFIC RELIEF PROVISIONS APPLICABLE TO PARTICULAR LAWSUITS AND SITUATIONS

SECTION A. *Interest in Excess of Six Percent per Year*

Let us assume that you entered into an obligation which requires you to pay more than six percent per year. Afterwards you enter the military service. Under the Civil Relief Act you may start paying, if you like, only six percent. However, you are advised to tell your creditors what you are going to do and cite the Act as your authority. If the person whom you owe objects, he must ask the proper court to require you to pay more than six percent per year. However, before the court requires you to pay interest in excess of six percent, the court must conclude that your ability to pay the higher rate is "not materially affected by reason of your military service."

As used in the Act, "interest" includes "service charges, renewal charges, fees, or any charges (except bona fide insurance) in respect of such obligations***"

CAUTION: This relief applies only to obligations made *before* you entered military service, not to those made while in the service.

SECTION B. *Installment Contracts, Mortgages, Trust Deeds, etc.*

While a civilian you entered into contracts to buy a home, a refrigerator, wristwatch, automobile, or perhaps even a horse. You paid so much down and agreed to pay the remainder in monthly installments. Under each contract you agreed, for all practical purposes, that if you failed to make the payments on the dates specified in the contracts, the seller could repossess the property and sell it to the highest bidder. Furthermore, you may have agreed, for example, that if at the time of the sale you still owed $1,500 and if the seller were to get only $1,000, you would still be liable to the seller for the $500 difference. While these contracts are in force you enter military service, and because of your reduced income you fail to make payments when due. Does the Act provide you with any protection?

Yes, but not to the extent of being unfair to the seller. Remember, we are talking about contracts you made and paid on *before* you entered the service. Under these circumstances the seller cannot repossess or foreclose on the property involved without first getting the permission of a court. If the seller were to take the property and sell it without a court's permission, he could be made to pay a fine and even be sent to jail. Before a court will give its permission, it looks into the reason behind your failure to make payments when due. If satisfied that such failure is attributable to your military service, the court will then do what it thinks is fair to you and to the seller. It may, for example, order you to return the property to the seller, and the seller to return to you the amount you have already paid. Or, it may decide to let you keep the property and make smaller payments than called for in your contract.

CAUTION: *This protection does not apply to obligations incurred after you entered into military service.*

SECTION C. *Leases and Evictions*

1. *Leases.* When you entered military service, you and your dependents were living in a rented house or apartment. You pay rent by the month. The lease still has a few months or even several years to run. You cannot, and your dependents do not wish to, remain in the house or apartment. Can you cancel the lease?

Yes, by giving your landlord thirty days written notice and citing the Act as your authority. The "thirty days" does not necessarily start running from the day notice is given. Rather, it starts running on the day the next monthly rent payment is due. For example, you pay rent on the first of each month. You give notice on the 20th of October. In this case, you owe rent for November. Your lease terminates on the last day of November.

The Act has a special "notice" provision for leases requiring rent to be paid other than by the month.

The right to terminate leases under the Act includes not only property leased and occupied for dwelling purposes but also property leased and occupied for "professional, business, agricultural or similar purposes."

CAUTION: A common misconception about the Act is that is authorizes a servicemember to terminate a lease made *after* he has entered the service—*it does not*. This means that a lease made *while* you are in service should contain a clause providing for termination on thirty days written notice if you receive transfer orders.

2. *Evictions.* Your dependents (wife, children, parents, etc.) are living in a house or apartment for which the rent is *$150 or less* per month. The rent is not paid. Can they be evicted?

Yes, but only after a court has given permission. This is so whether your dependents began living there *before or after* you entered military service. If the landlord evicts them without first securing a court's permission, he could be fined, placed in jail or suffer both penalties.

Once the landlord asks a court's permission to evict your dependents, the court first decides whether or not nonpayment of rent is attributable to the fact that you are on active military duty. If the court decides that your delinquency is not caused by this fact, then it may order your dependents evicted.

On the other hand, if failure to pay is attributed to your military service, the court will make the landlord wait for not longer than three months before authorizing eviction. The idea is to provide a reasonable time during which another place for your dependents to live can be found. However, the payment of all rents due is not thereby excused.

The landlord is also prohibited by the Act from holding your household goods as security for unpaid rent, unless permitted by the court.

PART IV.—MISCELLANEOUS PROVISIONS
SECTION A. *Insurance*

You are the owner of a commercial insurance policy insuring your life. On entering military service you may not be able to continue to pay the premiums because of your reduced income.

Under such circumstances, if you wish to keep the policy current and it has been in force for at least 180 days, you may, under the Civil Relief Act, request the Veterans Administration to guarantee payment of the premiums. The maximum amount of life insurance on which payment of premiums will be guaranteed is $10,000. That amount may be in one or more policies.

Upon separation from military service, you have 2 years in which to arrange with the insurer to pick up regular premium payments and pay any back premiums and interest. At the end of the 2 years, any remaining indebtedness is treated as a policy loan, unless the indebtedness exceeds the cash value. In the latter event, the policy is terminated and the VA pays the insurance company the difference between the indebtedness and the cash value. The amount paid by the VA then becomes the veteran's debt to the United States.

SECTION B. *Storage Liens*

Suppose either before or during your military service, you place your "household goods, furniture, or personal effects" in storage. You fail to pay the storage charges when due.

Under these circumstances, the storage company cannot sell your property to cover its charges without a court order. If your failure to pay is due to your being on active military duty, the court may stay the proceedings or enter a judgment that the court thinks is fair to both parties.

SECTION C. *Public Lands, Mining Claims and Homestead Entries*

Special provisions of the Act relate to mining, homestead and other claims on public lands. These claims will not be lost through absence resulting from your military service if you follow the applicable provisions of the Act.

PART V.—TAXES (AND MOTOR VEHICLE REGISTRATION)

SECTION A. *General*

The Civil Relief Act exempts your service pay and personal property from taxation by States in which you may be stationed other than your home or domiciliary State and also provides that the payment of income tax may be deferred for up to six months after discharge if your ability to pay the tax is materially impaired by reason of your service.

SECTION B. *Residence vs. Domicile*

1. *General.* Before you can determine what taxes are properly assessable to you and your dependents, you must understand the distinction between the terms "residence" and "domicile" and the protection afforded by the Act.

Under the Act the sole right to tax *your* military pay and *your* personal property remains with your State of domicile when you are absent therefrom in compliance with military or naval orders.

2. *Residence.* Residence may generally be defined as "a factual place of abode" at a particular time. However, a great deal of confusion exists in defining this term because various State laws define the words "residence" or "resident" differently. The definition of "resident" also differs in application of the tax laws of the various States. Whenever a word is specifically defined in a particular law, that definition is, of course, controlling.

3. *Domicile.* Domicile may be defined in legal terms as "that place where a man has his true, fixed and permanent home and principal establishment and to which, whenever he is absent therefrom, he has the intention of returning."

To understand the problem of domicile, you must first realize that a domicile may be determined by any one of the following criteria, namely, (1) domicile of origin or birth, (2) domicile by operation of law, and (3) domicile of choice. As a matter of law everyone has a domicile somewhere, and an old domicile is not lost until a new one is acquired.

Domicile of origin is the domicile automatically acquired by every child at birth and is identical with that of his parents. The actual place of birth may not determine domicile of origin. For example, a child born to citizens of the United States who are stationed in Virginia pursuant to military orders does not necessarily become a domiciliary of Virginia. If at that time the father was domiciled in Colorado, the child also becomes a domiciliary of Colorado.

Like domicile of origin, domicile by operation of law exists independent of the subject's intention and actual residence. For example, a woman upon marriage generally loses her own domicile and, by operation of law, acquires that of her husband regardless of her actual residence or intention.

Domicile of choice is the place which a person has voluntarily elected and chosen for himself to replace his previous domicile. To change domicile there must be a *simultaneous* concurrence of the following elements:

(1) actual residence (bodily presence) in the new locality;

(2) an intention to remain there permanently or indefinitely; and

(3) an intention to abandon the old domicile.

Once the above elements have occurred *simultaneously* you have changed your domicile. However, proving the requisite intent, particularly if the change of domicile gives you a tax advantage, may be difficult. In this event your word, though considered, will not necessarily satisfy taxing authorities. They may demand, and properly so, evidence of some overt acts on your part indicative of the requisite intent. In short, your actions speak louder than your words. Some of the clearest indications that you consider a State to be your domicile are registering to vote and actually voting there, licensing your motor vehicle, and paying income or personal property taxes, if any.

Service personnel are tempted from time to time to change their domiciles in order to avoid the income tax of a particular State. Before doing so, you should remember that domicile not only exerts its influence in determining your liability for income and personal property taxes but in other very important areas as well. The following enumeration is illustrative of these areas:

1. liability for State inheritance taxes;
2. the place where your will would be probated, who may act as executor thereof and as testamentary guardian of your minor children;
3. the right to vote;
4. bonuses for wartime service;
5. the right to hold public office;
6. the right to homestead, veterans claims, or tax exemptions;
7. whether you or your children may attend a State college without paying higher fees required of nondomiciliary residents;
8. where you may obtain a divorce.

In short, before attempting to change your domicile, take a good long look at the overall picture.

SECTION C. *Income Taxes*

As previously stated, the Civil Relief Act, a Federal law, *exempts* your military pay from all State income taxes except those imposed by the State of your domicile while absent therefrom in compliance with military orders. Therefore, unless your present duty station is located in the State of your domicile, your military pay cannot be taxed by the State where stationed even though its laws provide otherwise.

The Act does *not* except nonmilitary income derived from sources within a State where you may be serving. States can and do, for example, require you to pay an income tax on salaries from civilian employment therein, rents from real property located therein, and profits from the sale of such property, even though your domicile is elsewhere. Ordinarily you will file a "resident" income tax return in your home (domiciliary) State on *all* of your income and a "nonresident" return in the State where stationed on nonmilitary income earned in that State. This could mean that you may pay taxes on your nonmilitary income to both your home State and the State where stationed. However, credits may reduce the overall tax burden.

Furthermore, the Act does not exempt any civilian member of your household from taxes by the State in which he or she is temporarily residing. For example, if you are domiciled in Florida, ordered to duty in Virginia and accompanied by your wife (civilian) who obtains employment there, your wife is liable to Virginia for income tax on her salary from Virginia employment. See your legal assistance officer or income tax adviser for rules governing apportionment.

Any tax on income (Federal, State or local) may be deferred for a period extending not more than six months after separation from active service, without interest or penalty, if your ability to pay the income tax is materially impaired by reason of such service. You should make written request upon the taxing authorities for such deferment. Note that this does not excuse you from filing a return unless your home State law specifically exempts you from filing.

SECTION D. *Personal Property Taxes*

As the "tax day" varies from State to State, your personal property could be present for tax purposes in several taxing jurisdictions the same year. To protect you, the Act prohibits any State except that of your domicile from taxing *your* personal property, except personal property used in a trade or business.

It is emphasized that the Act does not relieve your wife from paying the tax to the State where residing on her personal property.

SECTION E. *Real Property Taxes*

Real property (such as a house) is subject to local taxes. The Act gives you *no* exemption from this tax.

SECTION F. *Motor Vehicle Registration*

The Act allows you to retain your home State registration on your motor vehicle as long as you have paid the license fee or excise required by your home State. The vehicle title should be in your name alone as the Act exempts only you.

PART VI.—CONCLUSION

The specific nature of all the relief available to you under the Act is a matter about which you should consult an attorney. The Act is designed to deal fairly with you and your creditors. While relief is very often available to you, you are expected and required to show good faith by doing what you can to discharge your obligations.

Chapter Thirteen
REGULATION Z— THE WAY TO WIN

"Don't look back, something may be gaining on you."
—Satchel Paige

Without a question, Regulation Z is the most feared threat a borrower can make to a lender, and with good reason. Under Regulation Z, the Truth in Lending law, it is possible for a judge to declare that a borrower does not need to repay interest on a mortgage! An agreement can be arranged whereby the borrower need not repay all of the principal originally borrowed. The lender might even be fined as much as *three times* the debt in damages!

Regulation Z is probably the most lethal weapon in a mortgagor's arsenal.

Yet today only a handful of borrowers have used it. In talking with one lender I heard the comment, "Yes, it works against us. But it takes a highly sophisticated borrower and a high-powered attorney to pull it off."

I don't think so. I think that Regulation Z is the average person's biggest answer when it comes to stopping foreclosure. I think we can all use it and once lenders realize we are willing to, the whole structure of foreclosure will change.

A WORD ABOUT LENDER'S RIGHT

It is very doubtful that the drafters of Regulation Z ever thought it would be used to stop foreclosure. Lenders point out with much justification that it just isn't fair for borrowers to use it against them. (In doing research for this chapter, I walked into a central office of one of the biggest banks in the country. I asked to talk with the man in charge, and everything was all handshakes and smiles until I mentioned Regulation Z. Then the man turned white, refused to say another word, and asked me to leave. That's how much lenders are worried about it!) Unquestionably, it's an unfair tactic.

But if it's your house, you're up against the wall, you're living in desperate times, and the lender won't be reasonable—

REGULATION Z

Regulation Z, the Truth in Lending law, was enacted by Congress and became law on July 1, 1969. It provides for certain procedures that *must* be carried out by nearly everyone who lends money. These include full disclosure of items such as the interest rate charged, the full amount of the loan, the full amount of the interest, and the annual percentage rate (APR). There even is a specific method of calculating the APR that *must* be used.

The law applies to lenders of money who extend credit more than twenty-five times during the previous year or more than five times in a year for transactions secured by dwellings. This simply means that it almost always applies to banks, savings and loans, and other institutional lenders. It applies less frequently to private lenders.

Although there are many provisions of Regulation Z that relate directly to consumers, we are concerned about the parts of the law that relate to real estate. Real estate transactions under Regulation Z are termed closed-end credit transactions. The meaning here is that the credit is offered for a specific time period. The amount of the loan, the costs, and the schedule for repayment are all agreed upon in advance.

The lender must reveal to the borrower the *exact* amount of the finance charge under Regulation Z. With regard to closed-end credit, or that found on real estate, the amount of the finance charge includes:

Interest on the mortgage
Transaction charges
Service charges
Loan fees
Mortgage insurance
Premiums for property insurance (if required by the lender)
Premiums for health or accident insurance (if required by the lender)

In other words, virtually all costs in the transaction are required to be considered finance costs. That's why when we get a mortgage for, say, fourteen percent, the APR might state "fourteen and one-half." The extra half-percent is what is being charged for the costs of closing the deal.

What might not be apparent on the surface here is the fact that calculating the APR can be very, very difficult for the lender.

Some of the costs, such as interest, may fluctuate, depending on when in the month the money was borrowed. Other costs, such as title insurance or escrow fees, may vary from title company to title company.

Usually the calculation of the APR is saved for the final day of the transaction, and then the calculation is made by an experienced member of the lender's team.

Nevertheless, things can go wrong for the lender (and right for the borrower who is in foreclosure).

For example there is the classic Campbell case, which occurred in southern California.

Here a borrower was negotiating a 500,000-dollar mortgage on a residence that he intended to occupy. The loan was arranged, all the documents were ready to sign to close the deal, and then the borrower backed out of the deal. It didn't close.

A few weeks later the borrower came back and said that he was now ready to sign.

The documents were made ready and once again, just as the signing was to take place to conclude the transaction, the borrower backed out of the deal. (Note: Why the borrower backed out is irrelevant to the story.)

Finally, for the third time, the borrower agreed to go through with it. This time the borrower performed. He signed all the documents.

What's the problem?

It's this. The escrow company, faced with having to draw and redraw documents, added in an additional fee of a little over 100 dollars for their extra work. This fee was clearly mentioned in the closing statement the borrower signed. *But it was never calculated into the APR.* The Regulation Z document the borrower signed did not reflect this amount.

A short time later the property was in foreclosure. The lenders thought they had a sure case—nothing could go wrong. But it did. The borrower hired an attorney, who went to court charging the lenders with violation of Regulation Z. The attorney claimed that the lenders had violated the law by not including that extra 100 dollars when calculating the APR.

A minor discrepancy, right? What's 100 dollars in a half-million–dollar mortgage?

It's a lot. Here's the eventual disposition of the case. After owning the house for many, many months, the lenders agreed to allow the borrower not to have to pay *any* interest at all! Even more astonishing, the borrower was only required to repay 400,000 dollars of the 500,000-dollar debt—100,000 dollars was forgiven!

I hope you're beginning to see the power of Regulation Z.

Any tiny error made in the documents may be sufficient grounds for halting foreclosure. In addition, Regulation Z provides severe penalties for lenders who make errors. These penalties include:

> loss of part or all of the interest due the lender
> fines of up to *three times* the amount loaned
> possible recision of the transaction

I was talking with a lender while writing this chapter. He commented, "Our liability is so great, the chances of making an error so large, that I don't see how we can make any second mortgages or safely make many "firsts." Yet we continue to do so. I hope the public never finds out!"

COMPLEXITY

What are the chances that the lender made an error on *your* documents?

Probably a lot better than you realize—Regulation Z is one of the most complex laws ever enacted. To help explain it *to lenders* the Board of Governors of the Federal Reserve System has two booklets.

The first booklet is entitled *Regulation Z Truth In Lending* and is 88 pages of tiny print. The second booklet is entitled *Official Staff Commentary on Regulation Z Truth in Lending* and is 103 pages of tiny print.

In addition, every major lender also has its own *Regulation Z Truth in Lending* handbook, which its loan officers use. Typically these handbooks are hundreds of pages long.

The fact that a book might be long is in itself not a completely convincing argument. To make the point, therefore, starting on the following page is Appendix J from the Federal Reserve's *Regulation Z Truth in Lending* booklet, explaining just how to calculate closed-end credit or the type used on real estate (this material occupies only five pages of the booklet).

I'm not a mathematical genius, but even if I were, I would have a tough time here. I think what should be clear is that given the complexity of the law, the variables involved, and the volume of mortgages put through by most lenders, the chances of error are very high.

WHAT TO DO

You're facing foreclosure. You're desperate. Now suddenly Hal Morris just maybe is throwing you a lifeline. How do you take advantage of it?

The first thing to do is to get hold of your Regulation Z documents. Assuming you received your mortgage after 1969 and you got it from an institutional lender, there have to be Regulation Z documents. (If there aren't, the lender, not you, is in real trouble.)

You will find the documents with the other papers you received when you purchased your property.

If you can't find your Regulation Z documents, go to your lender and insist on receiving copies. The lender should give them to you (and just your appearing and demanding them may give the lender a whole different perspective on how to handle your foreclosure). If for any reason the lender refuses, you can probably force the lender to give you copies of the documents by contacting the appropriate regulatory agency. Here are the agencies to contact for:

APPENDIX J—Annual Percentage Rate Computations for Closed-End Credit Transactions

(a) *Introduction.* (1) Section 226.22(a) of Regulation Z provides that the annual percentage rate for other than open-end credit transactions shall be determined in accordance with either the actuarial method or the United States Rule method. This appendix contains an explanation of the actuarial method as well as equations, instructions and examples of how this method applies to single-advance and multiple-advance transactions.

(2) Under the actuarial method, at the end of each unit period (or fractional unit period) the unpaid balance of the amount financed is increased by the finance charge earned during that period and is decreased by the total payment (if any) made at the end of that period. The determination of unit periods and fractional unit periods shall be consistent with the definitions and rules in paragraphs (b)(3), (4) and (5) of this section and the general equation in paragraph (b)(8) of this section.

(3) In contrast, under the United States Rule method, at the end of each payment period, the unpaid balance of the amount financed is increased by the finance charge earned during that period and is decreased by the payment made at the end of that payment period. If the payment is less than the finance charge earned, the ad-justment of the unpaid balance of the amount financed is postponed until the end of the next payment period. If at that time the sum of the two payments is still less than the total earned finance charge for the two payment periods, the adjustment of the unpaid balance of the amount financed is postponed still another payment period, and so forth.

(b) *Instructions and equations for the actuarial method.* (1) *General rule.* The annual percentage rate shall be the nominal annual percentage rate determined by multiplying the unit-period rate by the number of unit periods in a year.

(2) *Term of the transaction.* The term of the transaction begins on the date of its consummation, except that if the finance charge or any portion of it is earned beginning on a later date, the term begins on the later date. The term ends on the date the last payment is due, except that if an advance is scheduled after that date, the term ends on the later date. For computation purposes, the length of the term shall be equal to the time interval between any point in time on the beginning date to the same point in time on the ending date.

(3) *Definitions of time intervals.* (i) A period is the interval of time between advances or between payments and includes the interval of time between the date the finance charge begins to be earned and the date of the first advance thereafter or the date of the first payment thereafter, as applicable.
(ii) A common period is any period that occurs more than once in a transaction.
(iii) A standard interval of time is a day, week, semimonth, month, or a multiple of a week or a month up to, but not exceeding, one year.
(iv) All months shall be considered equal. Full months shall be measured from any point in time on a given date of a given month to the same point in time on the same date of another month. If a series of payments (or advances) is scheduled for the last day of each month, months shall be measured from the last day of the given month to the last day of another month. If payments (or advances) are scheduled for the 29th or 30th of each month, the last day of February shall be used when applicable.
(4) *Unit period.* (i) In all transactions other than a single-advance, single-payment transaction, the unit period shall be that common period, not to exceed one year, that occurs most frequently in the transaction, except that—
  (A) If two or more common periods occur with equal frequency, the smaller of such common periods shall be the unit period; or
  (B) If there is no common period in the transaction, the unit period shall be that period which is the average of all periods rounded to the nearest whole standard interval of time. If the average is equally near two standard intervals of time, the lower shall be the unit period.
(ii) In a single-advance, single-payment transaction, the unit period shall be the term of the transaction, but shall not exceed one year.
(5) *Number of unit periods between two given dates.* (i) The number of days between two dates shall be the number of 24-hour intervals between any point in time on the first date to the same point in time on the second date.
(ii) If the unit period is a month, the number of full unit periods between two dates shall be the number of months measured back from the later date. The remaining fraction of a unit period shall be the number of days measured forward from the earlier date to the beginning of the first full unit period, divided by 30. If the unit period is a month, there are 12 unit periods per year.
(iii) If the unit period is a semimonth or a multiple of a month not exceeding 11 months, the number of days between two dates shall be 30 times the number of full months measured back from the later date, plus the number of remaining days. The number of full unit periods and the remaining fraction of a unit period shall

From the Federal Reserve's *Regulation Z Truth in Lending* Booklet

Regulation Z Truth in Lending Booklet

be determined by dividing such number of days by 15 in the case of a semimonthly unit period or by the appropriate multiple of 30 in the case of a multimonthly unit period. If the unit period is a semimonth, the number of unit periods per year shall be 24. If the number of unit periods is a multiple of a month, the number of unit periods per year shall be 12 divided by the number of months per unit period.

(iv) If the unit period is a day, a week, or a multiple of a week, the number of full unit periods and the remaining fractions of a unit period shall be determined by dividing the number of days between the two given dates by the number of days per unit period. If the unit period is a day, the number of unit periods per year shall be 365. If the unit period is a week or a multiple of a week, the number of unit periods per year shall be 52 divided by the number of weeks per unit period.

(v) If the unit period is a year, the number of full unit periods between two dates shall be the number of full years (each equal to 12 months) measured back from the later date. The remaining fraction of a unit period shall be—

(A) The remaining number of months divided by 12 if the remaining interval is equal to a whole number of months, or

(B) The remaining number of days divided by 365 if the remaining interval is *not* equal to a whole number of months.

(vi) In a single-advance, single-payment transaction in which the term is less than a year and is equal to a whole number of months, the number of unit periods in the term shall be one, and the number of unit periods per year shall be 12 divided by the number of months in the term or 365 divided by the number of days in the term.

(vii) In a single-advance, single-payment transaction in which the term is less than a year and is *not* equal to a whole number of months, the number of unit periods in the term shall be one, and the number of unit periods per year shall be 365 divided by the number of days in the term.

(6) *Percentage rate for a fraction of a unit period.* The percentage rate of finance charge for a fraction (less than one) of a unit period shall be equal to such fraction multiplied by the percentage rate of finance charge per unit period.

(7) *Symbols.* The symbols used to express the terms of a transaction in the equation set forth in paragraph (b)(8) of this section are defined as follows:

A_k = The amount of the kth advance.

q_k = The number of full unit periods from the beginning of the term of the transaction to the kth advance.

e_k = The fraction of a unit period in the time interval from the beginning of the term of the transaction to the kth advance.

m = The number of advances.

P_j = The amount of the jth payment.

t_j = The number of full unit periods from the beginning of the term of the transaction to the jth payment.

f_j = The fraction of a unit period in the time interval from the beginning of the term of the transaction to the jth payment.

n = The number of payments.

i = The percentage rate of finance charge per unit period, expressed as a decimal equivalent.

Symbols used in the examples shown in this appendix are defined as follows:

Regulation Z Truth in Lending Booklet (continued)

$\ddot{a}_{\overline{x}|}=$ The present value of 1 per unit period for x unit periods, first payment due immediately.

$$= 1 + \frac{1}{(1+i)} + \frac{1}{(1+i)^2} +$$

$$\cdots\cdots + \frac{1}{(1+i)^{x-1}}$$

w = The number of unit periods per year.

$I = wi \times 100 =$ The nominal annual percentage rate.

(8) *General equation.* The following equation sets forth the relationship among the terms of a transaction:

$$\frac{A_1}{(1+e_1 i)(1+i)^{q_1}} + \frac{A_2}{(1+e_2 i)(1+i)^{q_2}} +$$

$$\cdots + \frac{A_m}{(1+e_m i)(1+i)^{q_m}} =$$

$$\frac{P_1}{(1+f_1 i)(1+i)^{t_1}} + \frac{P_2}{(1+f_2 i)(1+i)^{t_2}} +$$

$$\cdots + \frac{P_n}{(1+f_n i)(1+i)^{t_n}}$$

(9) *Solution of general equation by iteration process.* (i) The general equation in paragraph (b)(8) of this section, when applied to a simple transaction in which a loan of $1000 is repaid by 36 monthly payments of $33.61 each, takes the special form:

$$A = \frac{33.61\, \ddot{a}_{\overline{36}|}}{(1+i)}$$

Step 1:

Let I_1 = estimated annual
  percentage rate =   12.50%
Evaluate expression for A,
  letting $i = I_1/(100w) = $ .010416667
Result (referred to as A') =   1004.674391

Step 2:

Let $I_2 = I_1 + .1 =$ 12.60%
Evaluate expression for A,
  letting $i = I_2/(100w) =$ .010500000
Result
  (referred to as A'') =   1003.235366

Step 3:
Interpolate for I (annual percentage rate):

$$I = I_1 + .1 \left[\frac{(A - A')}{(A'' - A')} \right] = 12.50 +$$

$$.1 \left[\frac{(1000.000000 - 1004.674391)}{(1003.235366 - 1004.674391)} \right]$$

$$= 12.82483042\%$$

Step 4:
First iteration, let I_1
  = 12.82483042% and
  repeat Steps 1, 2, and 3
  obtaining a new I =   12.82557859%
Second iteration, let I_1
  = 12.82557859% and
  repeat Steps 1, 2, and 3
  obtaining a new I =   12.82557529%

In this case, no further iterations are required to obtain the annual percentage rate correct to two decimal places, 12.83%.

(ii) When the iteration approach is used, it is expected that calculators or computers will be programmed to carry all available decimals throughout the calculation and that enough iterations will be performed to make virtually certain that the annual percentage rate obtained, when rounded to two decimals, is correct. Annual percentage rates in the examples below were obtained by using a 10-digit programmable calculator and the iteration procedure described above.

Regulation Z Truth in Lending **Booklet** (*continued*)

(c) *Examples for the actuarial method.* (1) *Single-advance transaction, with or without an odd first period, and otherwise regular.* The general equation in paragraph (b)(8) of this section can be put in the following special form for this type of transaction:

$$A = \frac{1}{(1+fi)(1+i)^t} \left(P \, \ddot{a}_{\overline{m}|} \right)$$

Example (i): Monthly payments (regular first period)

Amount advanced (A) = $5000. Payment (P) = $230.
Number of payments (n) = 24.
Unit period = 1 month. Unit periods per year (w) = 12.
Advance, 1-10-78. First payment, 2-10-78.
From 1-10-78 through 2-10-78 = 1 unit period. (t = 1; f = 0)
Annual percentage rate
(I) = wi = .0969 = 9.69%

Example (ii): Monthly payments (long first period)

Amount advanced (A) = $6000. Payment (P) = $200.
Number of payments (n) = 36.
Unit period = 1 month. Unit periods per year (w) = 12.
Advance, 2-10-78. First payment, 4-1-78.
From 3-1-78 through 4-1-78 = 1 unit period. (t = 1)
From 2-10-78 through 3-1-78 = 19 days. (f = 19/30)
Annual percentage rate
(I) = wi = .1182 = 11.82%

Example (iii): Semimonthly payments (short first period)

Amount advanced (A) = $5000. Payment (P) = $219.17.
Number of payments (n) = 24.
Unit period = $\frac{1}{2}$ month. Unit periods per year (w) = 24.
Advance, 2-23-78. First payment, 3-1-78. Payments made on 1st and 16th of each month.

From 2-23-78 through 3-1-78 = 6 days. (t = 0; f = 6/15)
Annual percentage rate
(I) = wi = .1034 = 10.34%

Example (iv): Quarterly payments (long first period)

Amount advanced (A) = $10,000. Payment (P) = $385.
Number of payments (n) = 40.
Unit period = 3 months. Unit periods per year (w) = 4.
Advance, 5-23-78. First payment, 10-1-78.
From 7-1-78 through 10-1-78 = 1 unit period. (t = 1)
From 6-1-78 through 7-1-78 = 1 month = 30 days. From 5-23-78 through 6-1-78 = 9 days. (f = 39/90)
Annual percentage rate
(I) = wi = .0897 = 8.97%

Example (v): Weekly payments (long first period)

Amount advanced (A) = $500. Payment (P) = $17.60.
Number of payments (n) = 30.
Unit period = 1 week. Unit periods per year (w) = 52.
Advance, 3-20-78. First payment, 4-21-78.
From 3-24-78 through 4-21-78 = 4 unit periods. (t = 4)
From 3-20-78 through 3-24-78 = 4 days. (f = 4/7)
Annual percentage rate
(I) = wi = .1496 = 14.96%

Regulation Z Truth in Lending Booklet (*continued*)

National banks—Office of customer and community programs, Office of the Comptroller of the Currency, Department of the Treasury, 409 L'Enfant Plaza East S.W., Washington, D.C. 20219

State banks (which are members of the Federal Reserve)—Federal Reserve Bank serving the district in which the state bank is located

Banks who are not members of the Federal Reserve—Federal Deposit Insurance Corporation's regional director for the region in which the nonmember-insured bank is located

Savings institutions insured by the Federal Savings and Loan Insurance Corporation and members of the Federal Home Loan Bank Board system (savings and loan associations)—The Federal Home Loan Bank Board's supervisory agent in the district in which the institution is located

Most others—Division of Credit Practices, Bureau of Consumer Protection, Federal Trade Commission, Pennsylvania Avenue at Sixth Street N.W., Washington, D.C. 20580

These agencies will probably intercede for you to see that you get copies of your Regulation Z documents. They probably *will not* go to bat for you, however, if there is a minor error. This will probably be your own responsibility and your own cost.

Once you find the documents, look them over carefully. Starting on the following page are typical Regulation Z documents.

Even little things that seem perfectly all right can be errors. For example, one attorney I spoke with pointed out a case in which a second mortgage was made. The mortgage was for interest only and there was an impound account (for property taxes and insurance).

When filling out the form, there was a spot where it was necessary to list the dollar amount of the interest (after calculating the APR). Because of the fact that there was an impound, the escrow officer simply wrote "interest only," which was perfectly understandable.

Regulation Z, however, specified *dollar amount*. A permanent injunction was issued. It was three years before the lender could bring the case to trial and continue foreclosure. The lender abandoned the suit and the property. In this case Regulation Z actually permanently stopped foreclosure!

This is an important point to understand. An attorney I talked with

H-13—Mortgage with Demand Feature Sample

Mortgage Savings and Loan Assoc.

Date: April 15, 1981

Glenn Jones
700 Oak Drive
Little Creek, USA

ANNUAL PERCENTAGE RATE The cost of your credit as a yearly rate.	FINANCE CHARGE The dollar amount the credit will cost you.	Amount Financed The amount of credit provided to you or on your behalf.	Total of Payments The amount you will have paid after you have made all payments as scheduled.
14.85 %	$156,551.54	$44,605.66	$201,157.20

Your payment schedule will be:

Number of Payments	Amount of Payments	When Payments Are Due
360	$558.77	Monthly beginning 6/1/81

This obligation has a demand feature.

You may obtain property insurance from anyone you want that is acceptable to Mortgage Savings and Loan Assoc.. If you get the insurance from Mortgage Savings and Loan Assoc. you will pay $ 150⁻/year

Security: You are giving a security interest in:
☒ the goods or property being purchased.
☐ _____

Late Charge: If a payment is late, you will be charged $ N/A / 5 % of the payment.

Prepayment: If you pay off early, you may have to pay a penalty.

Assumption: Someone buying your house may, subject to conditions, be allowed to assume the remainder of the mortgage on the original terms.

See your contract documents for any additional information about nonpayment, default, any required repayment in full before the scheduled date, and prepayment refunds and penalties.

e means an estimate

H-14—Variable-Rate Mortgage Sample

State Savings and Loan Assoc.

Anne Jones
600 Pine Lane
Little Creek, USA

Account number: 210802-47

ANNUAL PERCENTAGE RATE The cost of your credit as a yearly rate.	FINANCE CHARGE The dollar amount the credit will cost you.	Amount Financed The amount of credit provided to you or on your behalf.	Total of Payments The amount you will have paid after you have made all payments as scheduled.
15.07 %	$157,155.20	$44,002⁻	$201,157.20

Your payment schedule will be:

Number of Payments	Amount of Payments	When Payments Are Due
360	$558.77	Monthly beginning 6-1-81

Variable Rate
The annual percentage rate may increase during the term of this transaction if the prime rate of State Savings and Loan Assoc. increases. The rate may not increase more often than once a year, and may not increase by more than 1% annually. The interest rate will not increase above 19.75 %. Any increase will take the form of higher payment amounts. If the interest rate increases by 1 % in one year, your regular payment would increase to $ 594.51 .

Security: You are giving a security interest in the property being purchased.

Late Charge: If a payment is late, you will be charged 5% of the payment.

Prepayment: If you pay off early, you ☒ may ☐ will not have to pay a penalty.

Assumption: Someone buying your house may, subject to conditions, be allowed to assume the remainder of the mortgage on the original terms.

See your contract documents for any additional information about nonpayment, default, any required repayment in full before the scheduled date, and prepayment refunds and penalties.

e means an estimate

REGULATION Z
DOCUMENTS

H-15—Graduated-Payment Mortgage Sample

Convenient Savings and Loan   Account number: 4862-88

Michael Jones
500 Walnut Court, Little Creek USA

ANNUAL PERCENTAGE RATE The cost of your credit as a yearly rate	FINANCE CHARGE The dollar amount the credit will cost you.	Amount Financed The amount of credit provided to you or on your behalf.	Total of Payments The amount you will have paid after you have made all payments as scheduled.
15.37 %	$177,970.44	$43,777	$221,548.44

Your payment schedule will be:

Number of Payments	Amount of Payments	When Payments Are Due
12	$446.62	Monthly beginning 6/1/81
12	$479.67	" " 6/1/82
12	$515.11	" " 6/1/83
12	$553.13	" " 6/1/84
12	$593.91	" " 6/1/85
300	varying from $637.68 to $627.37	" " 6/1/86

Security: You are giving a security interest in the property being purchased.

Late Charge: If a payment is late, you will be charged 5% of the payment.

Prepayment: If you pay off early, you
☒ may ☐ will not have to pay a penalty.
☒ may ☐ will not be entitled to a refund of part of the finance charge.

Assumption: Someone buying your home cannot assume the remainder of the mortgage on the original terms.

See your contract documents for any additional information about nonpayment, default, any required repayment in full before the scheduled date, and prepayment refunds and penalties.

e means an estimate

REGULATION Z DOCUMENTS

said, "Regulation Z is an almost perfect defense against foreclosure."

If you can't find any errors, don't despair. What I'm getting at is that you probably won't be able to determine whether or not there's an error in your Regulation Z form by yourself. (If the lender who's experienced at it didn't notice, will you?)

The next step is to make a decision. Does the chance that there might be an error justify the cost of finding out? Going to an attorney who can handle Regulation Z will cost money up front. If it turns out that there are, in fact, no errors, this might be money wasted.

If, however, you decide to take the risk, then gather up the forms along with all the documents involved in the transaction and go to an attorney in your area who works with real estate transactions. (When calling attorneys be sure to determine where their area of expertise is. You don't want an expert in personal injury handling your real estate case.)

(Note: Even if it's questionable whether or not anything is wrong with the documents, Regulation Z can be used as a delaying tactic to slow down foreclosure. Because of the liability involved, some lenders faced with a Regulation Z lawsuit will choose to abandon the foreclosure or reduce the mortgage amount. Of course what we're talking about here is negotiation between lender and borrower. The effect of the Regulation Z lawsuit might be to convince the lender to negotiate to abandon or reduce the loan; the lawsuit itself might not accomplish this.

One attorney I spoke with said Regulation Z was like blackmail. A borrower in foreclosure can use it to blackmail a lender.

SHOULD YOU USE IT?

Obviously we're talking about a different use for Regulation Z than the law originally intended. Mortgages are voluntarily taken out. If we take out a mortgage, and we really aren't cheated, then we should repay.

But times and circumstances change.

If I found out that financially my back was to the wall, I wouldn't hesitate to talk with the lender and explain the trouble I was having. (See the chapter on negotiating with a bank or savings and loan.) I suspect most lenders would grant me some kind of forbearance.

On the other hand, if the lender won't negotiate, talk, or be reasonable, then I would use all the weapons in my arsenal to combat the foreclosure. Regulation Z would be my big gun. I wouldn't hesitate to mention it to the lender. Personally, I would pay the fee an attorney would charge to see if there were any errors in my Regulation Z documents.

Of course, I can't really tell you what you should do beyond this: If you're in foreclosure, you should have legal advice. You should consult with an attorney.

Show your attorney this chapter. Ask your attorney what he or she knows about Regulation Z. If your attorney doesn't know about it, maybe he or she knows of a specialist in your area who does. Ask your attorney if you should pay an expert attorney to have your documents examined.

Your best bet is to consult with your attorney to see if Regulation Z can be the answer to your stopping foreclosure—remember, if the lender made an error you might be entitled to treble damages. One borrower found an error and wound up paying no interest on his loan—and even had the principal amount reduced by 100,000 dollars!

Chapter Fourteen
BANKRUPTCY—
IS IT WORTH IT?

"Bankruptcy in the 1980s: Our biggest growth industry."
—one of the most popular seminars of the American
Bar Association annual national convention

There was a time not too long ago when a person who declared bankruptcy was looked upon as a failure. In some circles such a person was even regarded as a kind of thief, someone evading creditors to whom he or she owed legitimate debts.

In the recent economic climate, that has all changed. Today there are probably more people in one form of bankruptcy or another than during the Great Depression. (We can't know for sure because accurate records weren't kept then.)

In a way it's kind of like divorce. Not that many years ago, people who divorced had a certain stigma attached to them. But so many people have become divorced that today it's not considered in the least out of the ordinary. In the future, a person speaking of having been in bankruptcy during the early 1980s will simply get a sympathetic nod of the head and a comment such as, "You, too, eh?"

WHY BANKRUPTCY?

Bankruptcy is a legitimate means of avoiding being swamped by debt. Some of the most successful people in our country, at one time or another, resorted to bankruptcy. The list includes Walt Disney, Jerry Lewis, Ulysses S. Grant, and P.T. Barnum!

According to one judge who sat for years in bankruptcy court, the major reasons people file bankruptcy, in their order of frequency, are:

1. Creditor pressure
2. Loss of job
3. Divorce or separation
4. Illness and accompanying inability to work
5. Personal business failure
6. Medical expenses
7. Lawsuits

To that list might be added a new reason that is rapidly becoming popular—foreclosure.

(I want to point out that declaring bankruptcy to stop foreclosure really isn't fair to a lender. But then, life's not fair, and if you're desperate—)

SEE AN ATTORNEY

A special word of caution: Don't rely on what you read in any book. Bankruptcy can affect your credit for years. *Don't file bankruptcy unless you are doing so on the direct advice of your attorney.* Unless you are an attorney yourself, you probably aren't qualified to determine if it is the right thing for you.

BANKRUPTCY AND FORECLOSURE

Although it usually doesn't permanently end foreclosure, bankruptcy can interrupt the foreclosure procedure. We can gain months and many times, years without losing our property.

Lenders who hold what they think are perfectly secure trust deeds and notes are often astonished to learn that they are prevented from foreclosing because the borrower has filed for bankruptcy. The

151

bankruptcy proceedings have the effect of freezing all creditors' actions until they can be sorted out. This includes foreclosure. We might be one day away from an auction sale; if we file for bankruptcy, that sale almost automatically is stayed.

THE NEW BANKRUPTCY LAW

The bankruptcy law was significantly changed in 1979, making it far easier than before for people to file. The rate of bankruptcies increased accordingly. In early 1982, however, the Supreme Court in effect ruled that the bankruptcy law was unconstitutional. As of this writing we are still awaiting action by Congress to change the law to bring it into accord with the Constitution.

Although the new bankruptcy law certainly will be different from the old, the staying of foreclosure upon filing probably will not be changed. Therefore it is worth dealing with more closely. (Note: The following discussion deals with the law as it was prior to 1983. For changes you should check with your attorney.)

THE PROCEDURE

When a person files for bankruptcy, he or she is asking the court for help. The assumption is that creditors are overwhelming the person and immediate relief is needed. The court provides that relief by restraining or prohibiting creditors from taking *any* further action. That includes preventing a lender from proceeding with a foreclosure regardless of where in the process it happens to be.

Of course, the mortgage lender has options. To reinstate the foreclosure, the lender can petition the bankruptcy court. The lender can point out that the mortgage is a loan voluntarily placed on the property by the borrower and secured entirely by the property; hence it should be considered aside from other debts the borrower may have. The lender might suggest that the only reason the borrower is filing bankruptcy is to avoid or slow down foreclosure. The lender might have other arguments.

The court judge will listen to the lender's arguments and if they are persuasive might issue an order allowing the foreclosure to procede.

So what's the point? What has the borrower gained?

Time—the biggest single advantage of bankruptcy is time. It takes time for the lender to petition the court. It takes time to get a judge to hear the lender's arguments. If the borrower replies to those arguments it takes more time.

During all that time the property is held in a kind of limbo. The lender cannot foreclose. The borrower need not make any payments on the mortgage to avoid foreclosure.

In the end the borrower may lose in court. At that point, depending on state law, the lender may either continue on in the process or may need to go back several steps, perhaps even to the beginning. Once again, time has been gained.

The amount of time varies, depending on court case load and local statutes. But a minimum of three months and a maximum of about three years are not unrealistic.

You might win!

We've made the assumption, thus far, that filing bankruptcy is *only* a delaying tactic. There is another possibility. The judge might see it our way.

Instead of simply filing for bankruptcy, we might turn around and sue the lender! Maybe we were lied to by the lender when the mortgage was placed on the property. Perhaps the terms weren't fully and fairly presented to us. It might have been that the lender made serious errors in the documents.

For reasons such as these, the judge might see fit to issue a permanent injunction against the lender, preventing foreclosure for years. Ultimately, if we prevail, the lender might be forced to accept no interest, to accept less in payment than the amount borrowed, or to accept nothing! It is possible that bankruptcy and a resulting lawsuit could ultimately stop foreclosure entirely. (See the chapter on Regulation Z for more information on stopping the lenders and getting interest and principal reduced.)

HOW IT WORKS

As of this writing there are basically three parts of the bankruptcy law that are available to borrowers—Chapters 7, 11, and 13. In addition, bankruptcy can be filed either severally (that is, by a single person) or jointly (as by husband and wife). Finally, you can file for bankruptcy either as a real person or as a corporation. Each of these different areas of bankruptcy offers a potential option to the borrower.

Let's consider the story of Peter. Peter was an independent truck driver living in Los Angeles. He was in his late fifties and married. He had worked hard all his life and a few years earlier had bought a new home with a big, high interest rate mortgage.

Suddenly a severe illness struck Peter down. He was off work and had no income except state disability insurance, which barely paid for groceries. His medical bills were largely paid by insurance, but he had all the other expenses of living.

Peter's wife tried to find a job. But she was unskilled and there was a severe recession on.

Peter began borrowing to survive. For a time he lived off his credit cards. But his illness dragged on for more than a year and eventually he used up all his credit.

Now the banks who had given him the credit cards were after him. So, too, was the mortgage company. It had been lenient. Because Peter was ill, it had let him get behind six months in payments. But now they started foreclosure.

Peter went to see his attorney. Bankruptcy was recommended.

Peter's attorney first formed a corporation for him. This was something Peter had meant to do for a long time, since he was an independent trucker, but had never gotten around to. The attorney placed the house into the corporation, and then had the corporation file for bankruptcy under Chapter 11. (We'll discuss the meanings of the different bankruptcy chapters in a few moments.)

The creditors were immediately stayed from taking action. The mortgage lender, however, petitioned the court to be allowed to continue foreclosure proceedings. The court agreed. *Time gained— two months.*

Peter's corporation now filed a new bankruptcy petition, this time under Chapter 7. Immediately the foreclosure procedure was stayed again.

Once again the lender had to go to court to petition to have the stay removed. Once again the lender persevered. *Time gained— three months.*

At this point, Peter's attorney had him transfer title to the house back to his own name and Peter filed bankruptcy under Chapter 13. Of course, there was an immediate stay of the foreclosure.

The routine was similar. The lender's attorney petitioned the court and the foreclosure was allowed to resume. *Time gained—two months.*

Then Peter himself filed bankruptcy under Chapter 7, and the whole process again occurred. *Time gained—another two months.*

Once the judge lifted the order, the attorney had Peter's wife file bankruptcy under Chapter 13 and then, afterward, under Chapter 7. *Time gained—five months.*

During the various bankruptcy filings, Peter gained a total of fourteen months. During that time he recuperated and got back to work. He was also able to arrange for a payback of his credit cards and so avoided trouble with the credit card banks.

Note: Although Peter *filed* for bankruptcy six different times and six different ways, he was never declared a bankrupt. His assets were never sold and his debts were never discharged. It is possible to *file* any number of times and then withdraw the bankruptcy request. As soon as the mortgage lender succeeded in getting a withdrawal of the foreclosure stay, Peter's attorney withdrew the request for bankruptcy. No bankruptcy judgments, therefore, were ever filed against Peter.

Although the filings did go on record against him, he had rebuttals to them placed in his credit file, and he lost little credit.

Ultimately Peter was up and on his feet. He sold his house. He paid off the mortgage lender and had good enough credit to buy another property!

CAN YOU DO IT?

Can you do what Peter did?

It depends on what the bankruptcy laws are when you read this and on how good your attorney is. Remember, Peter was able to keep going largely because he was able to continue paying his attorney's fees.

For a person facing foreclosure and serious financial problems, bankruptcy is an option that should not be overlooked.

TYPES OF BANKRUPTCY

CHAPTER 7

Chapter 7 is general liquidation of a bankrupt's assets. This is done by having the bankrupt and his or her attorney inventory the bankrupt's assets and liabilities. These are then presented before a judge. If the judge accepts the inventory, the assets are sold and whatever is obtained is distributed among the creditors.

There are certain exemptions to Chapter 7. These include:

1. house equity up to a maximum of 7,500 dollars
2. auto equity up to a maximum of 1,200 dollars
3. clothes, appliances, books, and other household items up to a maximum of 200 dollars for *each* item
4. 500 dollars in jewelry
5. tools of trade up to 750 dollars

If there is a joint petition, the amounts are doubled. (The equity in the house goes up to 15,000 dollars.)

Alimony and child support are not discharged by bankruptcy.

In addition, the procedure is fairly complex. If a bankrupt doesn't list a debt in his or her petition and a creditor doesn't file a claim, that creditor's claim might possibly follow through the bankruptcy.

Finally, bankruptcy can only be filed once every six years. This is a vital point to remember.

CHAPTER 13

Chapter 13 tends to be more attractive than Chapter 7. Unlike the case of Chapter 7, here the bankrupt doesn't always end up with a dissolution of assets.

Chapter 13 allows a bankrupt, with the aid of the court, to draw up a plan for handling all existing debts within three years. (In special cases the court can allow up to five years for repayment.)

The plan does not necessarily require that repayment be made *in full*. It can be a plan in which only a fraction of every dollar is paid.

Under Chapter 13, a trustee is appointed. (The trustee's fee is ten percent of the amount repaid.) The trustee watches over the affairs of the bankrupt and determines that the bankrupt is repaying according to the plan and is not wasting the remaining assets.

CHAPTER 11

Chapter 11 is very similar to Chapter 13. Chapter 11, however, is provided largely for the use of companies and corporations.

BANKRUPTCY AS LEVERAGE

We can sometimes use bankruptcy even without filing, if we use it as a threat. Remember the case of Peter and the way he delayed foreclosure by hopping from one chapter to another and from a corporation to himself to his wife?

Institutional and many private mortgage lenders are aware of this as well. Naturally enough, they don't like it.

A borrower might come into a lender's office and say something such as: "You've pressed me to the wall. I can't make the payments and I won't lose my property. I've contacted my attorney and she says that the best thing for me to do is file bankruptcy. She says I can file under several chapters—I can even form a corporation and file. If you won't grant me forbearance, you will force me to do this."

That's not the kind of thing a lender likes to hear. Most smart lenders will make every effort to get the borrower to change his or her mind. This usually takes the form of significant concessions.

DOES BANKRUPTCY REALLY AFFECT CREDIT?

In researching this question, I discovered some startling answers. According to a judge who asked to remain anonymous but who for years served as a bankruptcy judge, there are several things that can be done to preserve credit. Here are some of the things that he saw done to preserve a bankrupt's credit.

In one case, there days before the order staying a foreclosure was to be lifted, the person who was facing foreclosure formed a corporation with the address being the address of his house. Then the corporation filed bankruptcy.

This effectively tied up the house, preventing foreclosure from proceeding. When the lender attempted to foreclose anyway, protesting that the corporation and the entire bankruptcy proceeding was a sham, the court found the lender in contempt of court. The rule is that a lender may not procede with foreclosure once bankruptcy has been filed. It takes a judge's order to allow the foreclosure to move forward.

In another case, a married couple formed a general partnership just as a foreclosure sale was threatened. Then they bankrupted the partnership, effectively tying up the foreclosure. In addition, their names did not directly appear on the bankruptcy; rather it had the name of the partnership.

In another instance, a person filed bankruptcy, had foreclosure delayed long enough to sell the house, and then ultimately went all the way through to a discharge of the bankruptcy. It went on her credit report. But she had a job, making 25,000 dollars. She was immediately offered credit in the form of bank loans and credit cards. Her credit, it turned out, was better *after* the bankruptcy than before!

The general rule here is that if after bankruptcy you maintain a steady job earning 25,000 dollars per year or more, you probably can obtain credit cards and bank lines of credit within sixty days.

It can be a bit more difficult when you're buying a home. If you are well qualified for the mortgage, you probably have a good chance of getting it. On the other hand, if you're just marginally qualified, you might be turned down.

Chapter Fifteen
CAN YOU AFFORD TO OWN A HOME?

"Let us all be happy and live within our means, even if we have to borrow money to do it."

—Artemis Ward

Thus far we've made a big assumption. It's that the best alternative for us is to own a home.

Maybe that's not the best alternative for every one of us. Maybe it's really the case that given our financial condition, the state of the housing market, and the cost of financing, other alternatives make more sense for us.

Just because housing was the best investment in the country between 1976 and 1980, it doesn't mean housing is the best investment for you today. Maybe you really can't afford to own. Maybe the reason you're threatened by foreclosure is that you really are in over your head.

LOOKING AT HOW BUSINESSES OPERATE

We talked about income and expenses, cash flow, and net worth in an earlier chapter. There our thrust was to find out where we were financially. Now let's review that material briefly to find out where we *should be*.

Let's say that we are operating a real estate business where we are property owners. We have income and expenses. In real estate, income might come from rents. In other businesses, it might come from sales or merchandise. Expenses, in real estate, are things such as the mortgage, taxes, insurance, and so on. In other businesses, they are the cost of inventory and salaries.

If the income flow is larger than the expense flow, we are said to have a positive cash flow. For example, let's say we have an apartment building, and the building is bringing in 5,000 dollars per month. Our expenses, including mortgage payment, taxes, insurance, and so on, come to 4,000 dollars per month. We might say that our *positive* cash flow is 1,000 dollars per month.

On the other hand, let's say that our building is costing us 5,000 dollars per month in expenses. Our income is only 4,000 dollars per month. Here we are experiencing a *negative* cash flow situation.

Cash flow is positive when each month we end up with more money in our jeans. It is negative when each month we have to take money out to keep the business alive.

IN BUSINESS FOR OURSELVES

In today's economy it is very helpful to think of our own family as a business. There was a time in the United States when the average family made only about 5,000 dollars per year. But today, the poverty level is over 10,000 dollars, and the average family income is over 20,000 dollars. Many families with two breadwinners operate on an annual budget of more than 40,000 dollars. By comparison with just a few years ago, that's big business, and it should be treated as such. Each family should think of their finances in terms of a business. Just as in business cash flow is important, so, too, is it in families.

FAMILY CASH FLOW

In an earlier chapter, we spoke of credit and how to handle it. Our direction here is different. What we are concerned with here is how the mortgage on the family house affects cash flow.

The mortgage usually is the single largest monthly expense of the family. Let's say that a family has 2,000 dollars per month of disposable income (from whatever source). That's the amount that goes into the checkbook after taxes. That's the amount that the family can do with as they want.

Today, in many American households, nearly 800 to 1,000 dollars of that amount goes for the house payment. As much as half is eaten up by house payments. If the figure is 900 dollars, then that means there is only 1,100 dollars left for other expenses including utilities, clothes, food, entertainment, auto expenses, and so on.

It should be easy to see how the mortgage can have a big effect on the business of the family.

Today, with high mortgage payments, most families are in a negative cash flow situation. Lots of us bought a few years ago, making the assumption that inflation was going to continue indefinitely. The rules for buying in inflationary times were to buy at today's prices and pay back with tomorrow's dollars.

Well, for many of us, it's tomorrow, and the dollars we anticipated having to easily pay back mortgages just aren't showing up in any great quantities. Tomorrow's (today's) dollars are hard to come by. With the recession (some call it depression) it's becoming increasingly difficult for people to meet their family business expenses.

This is perhaps best seen in the case of the family that bought a home two years ago on which the payments are 1,000 dollars per month and the total disposable income is 2,000 dollars. They are paying half their total disposable income in a mortgage payment.

Government studies have indicated that the most a family can pay to mortgage payments (assuming they aren't wealthy) out of disposable income is one-third. That means that this family might be in trouble.

They knew that when they bought two years ago. But they figured they would scrimp and save for a few years and by then their house would be worth much more and their incomes would be much higher. As we've seen it just didn't work out that way. Perhaps the husband has had to take salary cuts just to keep his job. Perhaps the wife has discovered that her job is in jeopardy. Maybe their house simply hasn't gone up in value.

This family may be in a negative cash flow situation.

It might be that their income has been cut to 1,800 dollars per month. After house payments of 1,000 dollars, they might only have 800 dollars to live on. Even with cutting to the bare bone, it might be that their monthly expenses for food, clothing, and so forth (assuming they have several children) are 1,100 dollars per month.

$1,000	mortgage payment
1,100	monthly expenses
$2,100	
−1,800	income
$300	negative cash flow

In this family's business, the negative cash flow is 300 dollars. That means that each month, the family is spending 300 dollars more than they take in.

Where do they get that money?

It can come from a variety of sources. It could be that they have some savings, and each month they are reducing those savings by 300 dollars. It could be that they are borrowing on the family Visa or Mastercard account (thereby adding interest payments to their already tight expenses).

The whole point is that unless there's a light at the end of the tunnel, such as a big, new job with a huge salary or a chance to sell the house for a monstrous profit down the road, this is a no-win situation. Since in today's economy, a big salary increase or selling for huge profits doesn't seem exactly realistic, this family's negative cash flow looks as if it is going to lead them to financial ruin.

The best question they can ask is, "How do we reduce our negative cash flow?"

The best answer they can get (usually) is, "Reduce the size of your biggest expense." In other words, cut down that blasted mortgage payment. If they could cut their mortgage payment by 300 dollars (to 700 dollars per month), they could completely eliminate their negative cash flow. At 700 dollars per month, they would be breaking even. The question for the remainder of this chapter, therefore, is how to avoid a negative cash flow on the family business.

SOLUTIONS TO NEGATIVE CASH FLOW

STEP DOWN

This is the most obvious solution. Stepping down means bailing out of the property we currently own and getting into a smaller one. Smaller here means not only in size, but in monthly payments.

"But we need a house the size we have now for our family!"

Maybe you do, but do you need a bankruptcy more? These are tough times, and they often call for tough measures. Maybe it will be necessary to live in a smaller house for a few years until times get better and the family can expand again.

There are a variety of ways to step down. The cleanest is to sell the property we have and then buy another, smaller property. The problem here, of course, is that in today's market it is extremely difficult to get a sale. Nevertheless, for a person in a negative cash flow situation, trying to get a sale might be the best thing to do. If we have the money to handle the negative cash flow for a few months, let's list the property at a reasonable price and try to get rid of it. (Considering the negative cash flow situation we are in, it might be worthwhile to get out at almost any price just to get out of the negative.)

Another solution is to try to trade for a smaller house. This is increasingly difficult as more and more people face the problem of being in homes too big for them; nevertheless, it is something we should discuss with our broker.

DUMPING THE DOG

Selling (or trading) might be the best way out of our situation. If after examining our true equity (see Chapter 2 on how to figure out what our real equity is) it turns out that we have less than fifteen percent equity in our property, however, we might want to consider letting the house go to foreclosure.

If we can give a deed in lieu of foreclosure and thereby protect our credit, and at the same time get six to twelve months free rent, we might be able to get the equivalent of our equity out in saved mortgage payments. A thousand dollars per month that we don't have to pay comes to 12,000 dollars over a year; 700 dollars per month is 8,400 dollars per year. That's quite a nest egg to use when we get started again.

SELLING AN OPTION

Another way of immediately generating money that we can use to offset a negative cash flow involves selling an option to someone else.

In any market, even a bad one such as we have today, there are always investors around willing to bet on a turnaround. After all, just because real estate looks dismal right now, it doesn't mean that real estate will remain this way. There's a strong possibility, many say, that it could have a big turnaround. For example, demand for property is at an all-time high, even given the bad economic climate. The reason is that there simply isn't enough housing to go around. For the last several years, new housing has been way down compared to our needs, and very old housing is constantly being torn down. There are many who feel that this pent-up demand could be unleashed in a burst of buying the minute interest rates fall significantly.

This means that there are investors out there who are willing to bet on a turnaround. But usually they aren't willing to bet a great deal. For example, they are not usually willing to come in with twenty percent down on a house and get a new mortgage along with the negative cash flow it usually involves to take a chance on a possible turnaround in a few years.

On the other hand, these investors might be willing to spend a few thousand dollars if they can get the same possible return as they would by buying.

There's a way to do this, a way that can benefit you, the homeowner with a big negative cash flow. It's called an option.

An option is an old device that has long been successfully used in real estate. It is basically an agreement to do something in the future. For example, I own a home and I want to sell. You want to buy, but you won't be having any cash coming in for a year. So you give me 2,000 dollars on an option to buy my house at any time over the next year. Under the terms of the option, I have to sell to you *if* you come up with the money. I can't sell to anyone else. In exchange for giving you this privilege, of course, I get the 2,000 dollars of option money. If, at the end of the period, it turns out your expected money didn't materialize, then you don't have to buy. But you lose your option money.

In today's market, there are lots of advantages to investors to seek options on property. Without coming up with a lot of cash, they can *tie up today's prices.* If there is a turnaround in the future, they can later buy at what will then be an older price and resell for much more, making a significant profit.

Here's how an option might work. We might contact an investor and say, "I'll give you a two-year option to buy my house at today's prices [if no broker is involved, it's today's prices less commission]. In exchange, you agree to give me three hundred dollars per month (seventy-two–hundred dollars for two years) in option money."

What is the investor betting here? He or she is betting 300 dollars per month (which could be in the form of a 3,600-dollar payment for one year with a second-year option available for another 3,600 dollars) that he or she can sell that house for more than it's worth two years from today.

If houses go up in value after the recession ends, the investor could win big, really big. If they go down, of course, the investor's loss is limited to the option money—in this case a maximum of 7,200 dollars.

For us it's also a good deal. We, in one stroke, eliminate our negative cash flow. Suddenly here's a benefactor who's willing to cover our entire negative.

What's more, we don't end up losing our home. Instead we end up locking in today's price, which has got to be better than just dumping the property.

True, if in two years, prices do skyrocket, we stand to lose that big increase. But the way things are going with our negative cash flow, we would have lost our house long before that two years anyhow. Realistically speaking, we have nothing to lose and everything to gain by giving an option.

One point is worth considering. In an option, the investor is going to want to give as little as possible in option money. We, however, have to make our position absolutely clear. Unless we are getting at least enough to cover our negative, the option is useless to us. Unless the investor will pop for the amount we need, the option won't do us any good.

How to Find an Investor
Check your local paper. Investors usually advertise for property just like yours. As an alternative, consider taking out a small ad yourself, offering your property on an option.

Other good sources are title insurance companies and real estate brokers. They frequently know of people who are looking for just this kind of deal.

But beware! Once you give an option, you have committed yourself to sell. At the end of the option period, if the investor says, "Yes, I want to buy, here's the money," you can't turn around and say, "No, I've changed my mind." *Don't give an option unless you're prepared to sell.*

Where to Get Help
For more information on options, contact your broker or your attorney. (I also recommend my last book, *Crisis Real Estate Investing* [Harbor Publications, 1982], which has an entire section devoted to this use of options.)

RENT TO OWN
Another suggestion that some might consider is renting to own. This is just the other side of the coin from our last example. Instead of giving someone an option on your property, dump your property and get a lease/option on someone else's.

Consider this: If you can lock in today's price, does it matter whether you lock it in on your current property or on another one? For example, let's say you have a house worth 70,000 dollars. What about if you were to dump that house, move into another worth 70,000 dollars, and lock in that price on the second house? Aren't your chances of making money equal (assuming similar locations and houses) on either property?

Look at it this way. You have a negative cash flow (300 dollars in our example) that's killing you. So you let the property go to foreclosure (assuming you have less than fifteen percent real equity), saving your monthly payments to create a nest egg.

Now you go out and find a property to rent. Typically, in today's market, a house will rent for about thirty to fifty percent less than the amount of its total monthly payments (principal, interest, taxes, and insurance). That means that theoretically you should be able to rent a house as good as the one you are currently living in (with payments of 1,000 dollars per month) for about 700 dollars or less.

You dump your house, and then go rent the one next door for 700 dollars per month. Immediately, you've eliminated the negative cash flow.

But when we rent, instead of simply taking out a rental agreement, we insist on a lease/option. A lease/option can guarantee two things: First, we will not be kicked out (unless we don't pay our rent) for the term of the lease—usually one year or longer. Second, if we word it correctly, we can lock in today's prices. We can have an agreement that at the end of the lease period we will be allowed to purchase the property at a price fixed today.

This does two things for us. It eliminates the negative cash flow we were so concerned about before, and it gives us the opportunity to take advantage of any profits that might happen through a real estate turnaround in the future.

Caution: Tax Consequences

If you're considering a lease/option alternative, talk with your accountant or your tax planner first. There are some disadvantages here. For example, when we *own* a home, we are able to deduct taxes and interest from our state and federal income taxes. When we have a lease/option, we may or may not be able to do this (depending on whether the lease/option is considered a rental agreement or a sale). (Again, I suggest my book *Crisis Real Estate Investing*, which deals extensively with this concern.)

DUMP OTHER ASSETS

Finally, if our negative cash flow situation appears to be temporary, we can do some of the things suggested in an earlier chapter on credit. We can sell the motorcycle, the motor home, or the boat. We can hold a series of garage sales. We can try to sell enough of our assets to generate enough money to at least temporarily cover our negative.

Negative cash flow is one of the biggest problems people in foreclosure face today. But it doesn't have to be overwhelming. There are ways out.

You can:

1. sell an investor an option
2. take in a partner who puts up the negative in exchange for tax write-offs and future profit participation

Chapter Sixteen
IF ALL ELSE FAILS

"Many distressed sellers are waiting for their ship to come in. But if it ever did come in, they'd be waiting at the bus depot."

Let me recount an incident that is really a compilation of several similar occurrences rolled together.

Harry owned a home he had purchased during 1980 using creative financing. It had a "first," a "second," a "third," and a "fourth" against it, all at high interest rates. Harry was buried by the payments. He just couldn't make them.

Try as he might, he couldn't keep his house from foreclosure. He did everything, but the trust deed time clock was running out. Eventually his house was advertised, and the time came for it to be sold on the courthouse steps to the highest bidder.

In practice, of course, the sale occurs in a courtroom. I met Harry in that courtroom. We got to talking and he outlined for me what the financing on his home had been prior to the foreclosure:

"first"	$50,000
"second"	10,000
"third"	5,000
"fourth"	3,000
	$68,000

He said that he had put 10,000 dollars down, and that in today's market he figured it was worth about 60,000 dollars or 8,000 dollars less than it had been mortgaged for. He knew he had gotten a crummy deal when he bought, but he liked that house. He didn't want to lose the property, but paying on "first," "second," "third," and "fourth" was too much. He hadn't been able to keep up.

When Harry didn't make his payments, the lender of the "fourth" didn't start foreclosure. The lender figured the house must have enough equity to make it worthwhile for him. Even if Harry incurred the expenses of foreclosure, he would still owe more than it was worth. The holder of the "third" felt the same way.

The holder of the "second," however, considered. The house was worth 60,000 dollars. He held a 10,000-dollar "second" above a 50,000-dollar "first." Did it make sense for him to foreclose?

His costs of foreclosure would probably run several thousand dollars. Then he would take over the house and have to make payments on the existing "first" just to keep the property. If he tried to sell, he'd have the costs of sale including a commission. If all sales costs were ten percent, that was 6,000 dollars right there.

Ultimately the "second" holder decided it just didn't make sense to foreclose, so he let the property go.

That left the holder of the "first," a savings and loan association. The "first" holder foreclosed. After all, the savings and loan had 50,000 dollars to protect.

Harry contacted the savings and loan and said he wanted to keep his house. He simply couldn't handle it under the debt load it currently had. He could, however, afford the house *if* there were only payments on a "first."

The savings and loan was sympathetic. The last thing it wanted was to take back Harry's house in a depressed housing market. But it pointed out that there was little it could do. After all, it had no control over the junior mortgage holders.

It was then that Harry proposed a creative solution. He asked that at the sale, *if* no one else bid on the property and the savings and loan took it back for the amount of the "first," would it then turn around and sell the house back to him for the "first" plus costs (about 3,000 dollars in costs)?

The savings and loan agreed.

Thus Harry nervously awaited the auction.

When his house came up there were no bids. The savings and loan bought the house back for the amount of the first mortgage. Now the savings and loan owned it free and clear. As agreed, the savings and loan turned right around and deeded the house back to Harry, giving him a new mortgage of 53,000 dollars covering the old mortgage amount, lost interest, and costs.

Harry got his house and in the process permanently wiped out 18,000 dollars of untenable debt!

WILL IT REALLY WORK?

I left this story until the end of this book because it is about a last resort. Consider what might have gone wrong. The holders of the "second," "third," and "fourth" might have foreclosed. Someone might have bid as little as one dollar more than the existing mortgage at the sale. The savings and loan might not have gone along with Harry's plan. If any of these things had occurred, Harry would have lost.

But he didn't lose. The plan did work.

All of which is to say that *if* you cannot save your house from foreclosure, *if* it actually goes to sale, you still might not lose. There is always a chance that if you are shrewd, you might be able to buy your own property back at the foreclosure sale.

Of course, there are techniques other than the one Harry used. He might have arranged to come up with the money by borrowing from friends or relatives (unlikely). He might have arranged a new loan from another lender. The money could have been funded, and Harry could have been at the auction with a representative of an escrow company, holding a certified check to cover the required deposit in cash. In this case, Harry might have been able to borrow more than 50,000 dollars and thus have been able to outbid any other potential bidders on his property.

ENTER THE FORTY THIEVES

What we are seeing here is a last-gasp solution, an opportunity to pull victory out of foreclosure. Unfortunately it has one problem that we must consider, the forty thieves.

The forty thieves are so named by a kind of consensus within the real estate fraternity. They are an assemblage of speculators who follow auction sales. They look for a steal, and they usually have the money in cash to pull it off. They might block someone such as Harry from carrying off his intended victory. Let's consider how they work. (Again, the following example is a composition of many similar incidents I have seen.)

The property in this case was a single-family home being sold at a foreclosure auction. It was a trust deed sale, and so the auction was being held by the trustee. He began by reading the legal notice that had been previously advertised. It included the legal description of the property so that everyone present would be given notice which parcel was up for bid.

The mortgage on the property was a "first" for 60,000 dollars. Therefore the opening bid on behalf of the holder of the mortgage was 60,000 dollars.

The borrower was in the audience. He knew the property was worth close to 80,000 dollars. He had made arrangements with a savings and loan to have a new loan of up to 65,000 dollars put on the house. With him was a representative of the escrow company to arrange for the purchase, if the old borrower was the successful bidder.

The old owner offered 60,500 dollars on the next bid, 500 dollars more than the mortgage holder. He apparently planned on shutting out other potential bidders by thus increasing the bid amount.

For a moment the buzz of conversation in the room died down and it appeared the former owner would have the successful bid. But then, at the last moment, another bid came from out of a group of people across the room. It was for 60,525 dollars—25 dollars higher!

The old owner scowled at the new bidder and jumped the price another 500 dollars, to 61,025 dollars.

Almost immediately back came another bid—61,050 dollars!

The old owner looked worried. It was as if the new bidder were playing games with him. He decided to play back. He increased the bidding by 25 dollars himself, to 61,075 dollars.

This time the bid from across the room was an increase of 1,500 dollars, to 62,575 dollars!

Now the old owner looked worried. His maximum was 65,000 dollars. Here was someone who had jumped the bid by 1,500 dollars in a single whack. How much was the person willing to pay?

At this point, the new bidder came across the room to the old owner. Under his breath he said that he saw that the owner was under great emotional pressure to get the house back. Obviously it had been his home. The new bidder didn't want to hurt anyone. Yet he speculated in buying foreclosed property. If the old owner was willing to give him 500 dollars in cash so that his time wouldn't have been wasted, the new bidder would withdraw his last bid of 1,500 dollars higher and stop bidding. That would drop the price back down. For the 500 dollars the old owner would save 1,500 dollars and get his house. The old owner agreed and got his house.

Was this auction all on the up and up?

Not entirely: Would that new bidder have really bought the house if the original owner had stopped bidding?

I doubt it. Rules at most auctions say that not only can you increase your bid, but you can also take it back. The new bidder could conceivably have withdrawn his bids if the old owner stopped bidding. In other words, the new bidder might have made himself a 500-dollar profit without ever having intended to invest a cent! He did it by understanding and using the rules of the auction.

I have seen this used in a similar but somewhat different matter. A house is put up for auction. Immediately a new bidder offers one dollar more than the mortgage amount. An old owner is there and bids higher. Suddenly three or four other bidders seem to come out of the woodwork, and the price shoots up astronomically.

Eventually the old owner throws up his or her hands in exasperation and walks out. As soon as the door closes behind the old owner, the new bidders begin withdrawing their bids. Down the price comes until the only bid left is for one dollar above the mortgage.

The old owner was taken. The other bidders were acting together. They had decided to buy the property either together or by selecting one of themselves as a buyer. Then they simply used the rules of the auction to fool the only other real bidder, the old owner, into leaving.

These new bidders who act as I've indicated here are often called the forty thieves.

But, you might be wondering, doesn't the person who is holding the auction know what's happening? Why doesn't he or she take action to prevent this?

First of all, in some states it's not illegal.

Second, the person holding the auction is usually a trustee. He or she is probably a representative of a trust corporation whose job it is to sit and hold auctions. This person's motivation might simply be to get it all over with as quickly as possible. If he or she does have any loyalties, it is undoubtedly to the holder of the mortgage being foreclosed upon. This trustee wants to see that the mortgage holder gets the full money's worth. Beyond that, the person might feel no obligation at all to the old owner.

Note: Not all bidders at foreclosure auctions are like our forty thieves. Many are scrupulous businesspeople, other lenders, and investors. They are honest and hardworking and help make a market for foreclosed property.

AT YOUR SALE

Before the actual sale takes place see if you have any grounds to get an injunction to stop the foreclosure auction. For example, you could file a law suit against the lender or the seller if they used any undo influence or fraud when you got the loan. Did the seller tell you the property could be used for commercial purposes when it turned out to be residential? If so, you can file a law suit and a judge will issue a Temporary Restraining Order (TRO). This will stop the sale until there is a hearing before the judge. Ten years ago over fifty percent of all sales that were stopped were stopped by a TRO, (Temporary Restraining Order). Today, about seventy-five percent are stopped through the filing of bankruptcy action, and only ten to fifteen percent are stopped by TRO.

If you are unable to stop the sale and the sale takes place, always attend the sale. Take a witness with you, and take a tape recorder to record the sale. If there are any technical mistakes, the sale can be set aside. If they refuse to recognize bidders or there are any other goofs, you can still turn out to be a winner. Remember, any dollars in excess of your mortgage are going to come to you. The more spirited the bidding, the greater the odds that you might wind up with some money in your pocket. I know of one homeowner who attended the sale, did not disclose that he was the homeowner, and had another bidder pay him off not to bid on his own property.

If the sale does in fact take place and there are no mistakes, approach the real estate owned department of the bank and see if they will reinstate you as owner. I have seen sales where IRS liens, mechanic liens and judgements have been wiped out, and after the sale the bank reinstated the old owner, who was now able to continue to live in the property with much lower payments and obligations.

THE BOTTOM LINE

Above all else, don't give up if your home goes to foreclosure sale. You do have an opportunity to buy it back, if you act timely.

But don't get overconfident. Don't go to the sale absolutely convinced that you will come out triumphant. Even with the best of preparations you might still lose. Remember, bidding on your own house at a foreclosure sale is a *last* alternative.

If you fail, keep in mind that there will be other houses. Most of these probably will have better financing than the house you lost. If you lose, things could be worse—and maybe it's all for the best!

Conclusion
THERE IS HOPE

"The secret of walking on water is knowing where the stones are."
—Herb Cohen

It was just a few years ago that we all believed no one could lose money in real estate. The government would keep the inflation fires burning. Even if we made a mistake in judgment and bought a bad piece of property, it only meant waiting a little longer to sell and realize a profit.

Some people quit their jobs and bought and sold real estate for a living. Ads in the newspapers trumpeted the feelings of the day: "NO DOWN," "NO NEGATIVE CASH FLOW," "NO HEAD-ACHE, NO TAXES, NO WORK!" One ad said, "How I made $124,000 in 48 hours!" Maybe what we had been taught was wrong. Maybe there was such a thing as a free lunch. Real estate and the profits it offered became a national mania.

Then, almost as suddenly as it started, the decade of the dumb millionaire came to an end. Just when everyone finally believed, newspapers began to report a grim, new truth:

> Gone is the exuberance enjoyed in the late 1970s. In those days developers had problems of scarcity. They couldn't build

homes fast enough to keep up with buyers. In some cases they even set up lotteries to determine who got the privilege of making the purchase.

Today, hundreds of homes are vacant, without buyers or renters who can afford them. Prices have tumbled fifteen percent in the past eleven months alone. Only one builder in five is left in the business, most of the others having filed bankruptcy.

The grim news was felt everywhere. At one real estate investor's convention there were 1,300 attendees, and 1,100 properties were offered for nothing down. While doing research for this book, I found over 100 ads for foreclosures in one newspaper in one day. There are lots of other stories as well.

There is the couple in Long Beach, California facing foreclosure. The wife says, "We bought our home with a balloon payment figuring we could refinance when rates came down."

A young truck driver writes me, "I took out a 'second' on my home to get enough cash to save my truck. Now I've lose my truck and I'm about to lose my home!"

A woman writes, "I'm a stockbroker. I took this job so we could 'keep up with the Jones.' We bought a big house and now even with what I bring in, we're in foreclosure."

A Beverly Hills broker called me recently. He's got a prestigious Beverly Hills home. "But I'm in divorce proceedings and I just can't keep up the payments!"

All of these people are in foreclosure, and there are a lot more with similar stories.

Well over one million owners are currently delinquent in their payments by thirty days or more!

There are more people in foreclosure right now than at any time since the Great Depression. You might be facing foreclosure yourself.

IF YOU'RE FACING FORECLOSURE

If you're in foreclosure right now, you probably feel as if you're in quicksand. Everything you do, every twist and turn you make, only seems to get you in more deep. It might appear, ultimately, to be hopeless.

Don't despair. Help is on the way. If you are nearing foreclosure, you have a problem; but there is a solution to your problem. Any problem at all can be approached in one of four different ways. Here are the different approaches we can take:

1. THERE IS NO PROBLEM

This is denial. (I have been losing some hair since college, but for years any time my wife said anything about it, I would say, "No, I'm not!" One day I was blow drying my hair, and my wife said, "You are losing hair—"

"No I'm not!"

In exasperation she replied, "Then if you aren't, that sink is going through puberty!")

2. THERE IS A PROBLEM BUT THERE IS NO SOLUTION

In this we acknowledge there is a problem but give up looking at all the options that might solve it.

3. THERE IS A PROBLEM, THERE IS A SOLUTION, BUT I CAN'T FIND IT

4. THERE IS A PROBLEM, THERE IS A SOLUTION, AND *I CAN FIND IT!*

My approach in this book has been Number Four. There is a solution to your problem, and we can find it. There are lots of people who are finding solutions. Here is a letter I just received from a woman who had thought Number Three applied:

Dear Hal,

Just a note to let you know that I am making great headway against — Savings and Loan with my foreclosure problem, all thanks to the great input from your seminar. IT WORKED!

It really is amusing to watch the loan officer's body language and listen to the tone of voice when he figured out I knew what I was talking about . . . and then some. My attorney was able to contribute a couple of key points where they had not done their fiduciary duty to me with respect to notices as well as a possible Regulation (discrimination because I was a single female) violation at the time. I'm loving it!

She's winning. You can win, too, if you understand the rules of the game. Consider this story of what happened last year in one of the football championships:

The two teams were on the field as the game wound down to the *final four seconds*. For the team that was behind, it seemed hopeless. They were losing twenty-four to twenty. Their opponents had the ball on the losing team's forty-yard line and there were no time-outs left. All the team with the ball had to do was to run off four ticks of the clock, and their dreams of winning a state championship would come true.

The quarterback came up under the ball, took the snap from the center, and slowly started moving toward his sideline. His teammates and fans counted down with the clock: "Four. Three. Two. One!"

The fans and the band erupted from the stands, shouting and screaming. His teammates came out onto the field. The cheerleaders ran out hugging the players and were jumping up and down around the quarterback. One of the players from the other team even walked up and shook the quarterback's hand and congratulated him on winning.

But there was one fellow in that stadium who understood the rules of the game. The middle linebacker for the other team ran up to the quarterback, ripped the ball out of his hands, and ran sixty yards through the fans and the band down to the goal, where the referee signaled a touchdown!

The team that had no hope had won!

Why did they win?

The reason is that the quarterback didn't realize that the game wasn't over until he either ran out of bounds or fell to the ground and the play was called dead.

The point of this story is that it might indeed look hopeless to you. You might only have four seconds left to go before foreclosure. It might look as though there is no solution to the problem. *But if you know the rules of the game, you can still win.*

In addition to the rules, you need to know yourself. Here are personal pitfalls:

1. FEAR OF THE SYSTEM
One of the greatest threats to someone who is losing his or her home through foreclosure is fear of the system. The idea most people have is that the cards are all staked in favor of the lender. The lender has a big

building with marble columns in front. The lender has hundreds of people on staff including specialists in mortgages. The lender has it all.

The problem with the reasoning just described is that what it is really saying is that because the lender has all the muscle and all the knowledge, he also has all the power. Because the lender has the power, the poor little guy with the mortgage has to lose.

One of the most important concepts to have is: *Don't fear the system—use it.*

The truth is that knowledge is available to everyone. All it takes is the time and perseverance to seek knowledge out. That lender who has the big building and the huge staff also has many, many mortgages—probably a quarter or more of which are in some stage of foreclosure at any given time.

The truth is that no matter how big the lender's staff of people may be, that lender simply doesn't have that much time to spend on your individual mortgage. No lender has the time to carefully evaluate every individual mortgage from every legal aspect. It simply wouldn't pay the lender to hire a staff big enough to do that.

But if you're in foreclosure, you do have the time. You have hours, weeks, or even months to study your specific situation and to look for loopholes or mistakes. You have the time to gain the knowledge. Reading this book is a good starting point.

The situation is like the old story of the jailer and the prisoner. The jailer seems to have everything going for him. He's got the gun, the keys to the cell, and the club. He's got all the power, and the prisoner is powerless, right?

Not right: The prisoner has power because of his situation. Let's say the prisoner is a terrible wretch who's in for some heinous crime. The jail conditions are abominable. The food is bad, there's an open toilet in the cell, and the prisoner is desperately hungry.

Just outside the cell door the guard is eating a ham sandwich. The smell of that sandwich wafts in to the prisoner, who looks at the gruel prepared for him. He decides that what he wants more than anything else right then is half of the jailer's ham sandwich.

He calls his jailer over and says, "My food is not edible. Could I please have a piece of your sandwich?"

The jailer laughs. Why should he share his sandwich with the prisoner?

Again the prisoner asks politely and with respect. "Would you please share your sandwich with me?"

179

Again the jailer laughs, this time with a bit of irritation.

Finally the prisoner calls the jailer over and says, "If you don't share your sandwich with me in the next ten seconds I'm going to start banging my head against this cement wall. In a few moments I'll surely be bloody, perhaps even unconscious. When your captain finds out, I'll say that you beat me.

"Maybe I'll be believed, maybe not. But you'll surely have to answer to your captain and probably to an investigation. You'll have to spend time defending yourself and filling out forms, and it could be a blot against your record.

"On the other hand, you could avoid all that for half a sandwich."

The jailer makes a quick evaluation of the prisoner. He is in rags. He has no hope of getting out. His condition, in fact, is hopeless. Therein lies his power.

The jailer figures, "This guy has nothing to lose. He is just desperate enough to bang his head into the wall."

Do you think he got his sandwich? You bet he did. He discovered how to use the very desperation of his situation to gain power over his jailer. Similarly, when we're faced with an overpowering lender, our very situation can give us the means to act, if we figure out wherein lies our leverage.

2. PANIC

Another great threat to someone facing foreclosure is panic. Foreclosure is always accompanied by a deadline. It has a definite termination point. You can keep your house only until the foreclosure process is complete. Then, on a certain date at a certain time of the day, you lose.

It's like having a death sentence hanging over us. It occupies our mind. The most common way of reacting to this is to focus on the negative things that are going to happen. "My goodness, I'm going to lose my house! Isn't that terrible? I'll have no place to stay. I'll lose all my money. My gosh, my gosh. What shall I do?"

(It's kind of like Chicken Little running around yelling, "The sky is falling!")

Yet those who keep their heads say, "Fine, I'll put it back together and sell it at a profit!"

Panic is not a solution. It's part of the problem. Panic is the inability to take rational action. If we focus on all the terrible things that can happen, we are sure to panic.

How to Avoid Panic

Here are nine things we can do to avoid panicking when we're faced with foreclosure. Try them. They work!

1. Get away for a while—the worst thing we can do when things go wrong is to wallow in the problem. Usually we get ourselves so tied up we can't see the forest for the trees. Our imagination blows things out of proportion, and we go off the deep end. Getting away, even for a short time, puts things back into perspective.

2. Talk it over—almost always there's someone we can talk with. It could be our spouse, a friend, or a coworker. Just expressing our worry and our fear to another person forces us to put them into words. Any time we define a concern, it gives us a measure of control over it. If we have control, then we won't panic.

3. Don't blow your top—getting upset and blowing up can be a kind of pattern we can fall into. It is beneficial in that it relieves, temporarily, internal pressures. But it almost never leads to long-term solutions. Rather than blowing up, take your anger out somewhere else. Run a few miles or play a fast game of raquetball. You'll feel better and you won't have the guilt associated with blowing up.

4. Put things in their order—we are all often defeated by the apparent immensity of our problem. It's easy to say, "Oh, I can't possibly do anything because the problem is so big."

We're probably right. It is big. But we can always cut it apart into its pieces. We can find one piece that we can work on and that we can do something with. If we work on it and get a feeling of accomplishment, we then have the courage to tackle another piece, and so on and so on, until the immense problem is whittled down to size.

5. Give something to somebody else—the idea here is to stop worrying about ourselves all the time. If we put in some time at a convalescent hospital or help the needy in some way, we come to realize two things. First, everybody has problems. Second, the problems of others can be far worse than our own.

6. Get regular recreation—this is different than getting away from it all for a short while. Regular recreation is necessary for our mental health. It gives us a regular place to go where we can be away from our concerns. This is a continuing source of rejuvenation.

7. Don't take it out on yourself—you're not perfect. You weren't made that way. You do make mistakes. It's part of the game. If you expect perfection from yourself, you'll be disappointed, and when something really goes wrong, like foreclosure, you'll panic.

Take it easy. Look at all of your accomplishments. Don't get yourself down. Don't feel it's a personal catastrophe if things don't work out this time.

8. Build your confidence—we do this by convincing ourselves that we will indeed find a solution. One way of accomplishing this is what you are doing right now. You are reading a book that will give you specific information on what you can do to avoid foreclosure. You are getting knowledge, and knowledge is power. A person with power can negotiate a solution with confidence.

9. Get away from negative thinkers—I'm sure you're familiar with negative thinkers. They are the sort of people who take a look at your situation, shake their heads, and say, "It's hopeless." A negative thinker is that player on the losing football team who went up and shook the hand of the quarterback on the other team. A negative thinker is the person who throws in the cards in a poker game before the other person shows his or hers. A negative thinker says, "My *perceptions* of the situation are such that I'm sure I can't win." A negative thinker is convinced he or she can't negotiate an extension of a mortgage with a lender, and so the negative thinker does not try to negotiate an extension and so doesn't get an extension—a self-fulfilling prophecy.

Get away from anyone who doesn't believe you are going to succeed. The negative attitude will drag you down. That person's pessimism will prevent you from coming up with the creative strategy that will save your property.

To avoid foreclosure, you need to avoid panic. When panic does set in, remember the previous nine remedies.

3. GUILT
You can't make the payments, so you deserve to lose the property. The introduction to this book very clearly outlines how ridiculous believing this is in today's economy. You are not to blame for losing your house. If you have any doubts, reread the introduction.

4. PRECONCEIVED NOTIONS
"The bank won't listen." "The savings and loan would never accept that." "I have no bargaining power."

Have you used those expressions? If you have, then you have given sway to preconceived notions. You have come to believe that something can't be done even before you've tried it. Perhaps someone, a friend or a financial adviser, has said that a strategy you have in mind won't work. *You* believed them. You didn't try the strategy. You didn't check it out with other friends or financial advisers. You believed that because you had a preconceived notion it probably wouldn't work—and you made sure it didn't work.

Throw away your preconceived notions. When it comes to mortgages, the rules of the game are being written right now by people like you. Creative solutions are being found by borrowers and lenders across the country. There are those who give in to what other people say, and then there are those who go out there and find a solution to their problems.

5. BAD ADVICE

It is critical that you find a good attorney who has had experience with stopping foreclosures. Here are some steps to follow:

1. Don't get involved with a negative, "won't work" type.

2. Call five real estate offices and ask for their owners or managers. Tell them you are having a temporary problem and ask if they could recommend a good real estate attorney.

3. Call your local bank or savings and loan and ask for attorney referrals.

4. Call attorneys and interview them. Introduce yourself and tell the attorney briefly the area of your problem. A typical scenario begins with a phone call:

"Hi. I'm —. The reason for my call is I have been referred to you by — and I'm facing a foreclosure problem and would like to visit with you for just a few minutes. Is now a good time or would you prefer I call you back this afternoon at, say, 2:00?"

If now is a good time to talk, ask the following questions:

1. Have you handled foreclosures before? approximately how many?

2. Are you familiar with Regulation Z? Could you briefly explain how it relates to foreclosure?

3. Are you familiar with the Soldiers' and Sailors' Civil Relief Act? Can you tell me how it relates to foreclosure?

4. Have you handled many bankruptcies? approximately how many?

5. Would you or a less experienced member of your firm be handling my case?

You can get a pretty good feel for an attorney by his or her answers to these questions.

There are all kinds of attorneys. Some are fresh out of law school and don't know all the rules of the game that well yet. Others have been around for ages, but they might not have specialized in real estate law. Even the attorney who specializes might simply have always represented lenders before and might not know of the many creative solutions available. Remember, attorneys generally are not paid to be creative problem solvers.

This is not to slam attorneys. It is to point out that an attorney is not sacred. If you don't get good answers, see a different attorney. Where the loss of your home is involved, plan on interviewing at least three attorneys.

6. THE SENSE THAT ALL IS LOST

The final cause of losing to foreclosure is the feeling that it is all hopeless. Hopelessness acts to paralyze us.

I've seen real hopelessness. I've seen a deer being stalked by wolves. The deer knew the enemy was nearby and was alert. But the deer made the wrong move, and one of the wolves jumped and bit the deer on the hindquarter.

The deer was still all right. It was on its feet, and it wasn't badly injured. But it felt that all was lost. So it sat down in the snow.

Instantly half a dozen wolves were on it, chewing away on the still living deer.

That's hopelessness, and that's what it can do to us if we let it take control.

The way out from hopelessness is to have a plan that we believe can succeed. If we see a way out, then by definition the problem isn't hopeless.

"Hal," you might be saying, "that sounds good. But my situation *really* is hopeless."

Is it really? Here are some options open to you. Have you considered them yet?

1. Ask the lender to discount your loan for an early payoff.

2. Threaten the lender with court action for not making full disclosure initially under Truth in Lending.

3. Have HUD take over your FHA mortgage, give you a breather with no payments, and then reduce the payments you have to make.

4. Threaten the lender with an injunction.

5. Use the Soldiers' and Sailors' Civil Relief Act.

6. Sell other assets; get a new job.

7. File bankruptcy to immediately stop foreclosure.

8. Ask for forbearance from the lender.

9. Sell, trade, or refinance.

10. Take in an equity partner.

11. Sell the land and lease back the improvements.

There you are—eleven quick options to consider. Have you really thought about them before?

The point is, if you're feeling that all is lost, grab onto one (or more) of those solutions I've just listed and think about it. It might very well be your way out. It can be your light at the end of the tunnel. It can be part of your plan to succeed. As I noted before, if you have a plan that you believe will succeed, then by definition, the situation can't be hopeless.

There is hope. My goal in this chapter has been to perk you up and to get you off the floor, standing upright and ready to roll up your sleeves and go to work. You can only succeed in anything if you have a positive attitude. The whole point here is to get that positive attitude.

Remember, people lose to foreclosure because:

1. They fear the system.

2. They panic.

3. They lack knowledge.

4. They're afraid to ask.

5. They have preconceived notions.

6. They sense that all is lost.

7. They get bad advice.

You can accomplish more than you have ever dreamed possible. If there only ten words that I could give you that could help you in your current situation they would be: **If it is to be, it is up to me.**

PRICE LIST

1. **The Foreclosure System**
   Hal Morris' live two-day seminar on how to profit buying fore-closure properties. Includes a workbook. How to buy before foreclosure, during foreclosure, at the auction, and buying from lenders after the auction   **$275.00**

2. **Money Making Ideas**
   Six tapes full of money making ideas that work. Included are the "$200,000" idea; how to buy foreclosure and distressed proper-ties   **$69.50**

3. **Financial Independence with Rental Homes**
   Six hours of tapes of Hal's seminar on training top real estate professionals how to develop financial independence for their clients using his five year plan   **$69.50**

4. **Creative Financing in a Tight Money Market**
   This six hour album of Hal's unique financing ideas has helped thousands of agents and investors buy properties they never dreamed possible   **$69.50**

5. **Real Estate Superstars**
   Exciting live interviews with those select few at the very top, finding out their success stories   **$69.50**

6. **Equity sharing "An Answer for the Eighties"**
   A comprehensive manual with legal forms, partnership agree-ments and complete script for one hour seminar on this new and intriguing subject.
   Everything you need is here!   **$350.00**

7. **How to Syndicate Single Family Homes and Condos**
   Six hours of tape of a live "How to" seminar with all the forms and documents you need to get started now. Forms include partner-ship agreement, offering circular, prospectus, subscription agreement and much more!   **$69.50**

To Order, See Form on Next Page

ORDER FORM

(These Materials are Tax Deductible)

To order call (213) 577-7444 with a Master Charge
or Visa number or mail a copy of this form to
Hal Morris Companies, 175 S. Los Robles Ave.,
Pasadena, CA 91101

Please send me:
(Number of copies)

- ☐ **1. The Foreclosure System,** $275.00 each.
- ☐ **2. Money Making Ideas,** $69.50 each.
- ☐ **3. Financial Independence with Rental Homes,** $69.50 each.
- ☐ **4. Creative Financing in a Tight Money Market,** $69.50 each.
- ☐ **5. Real Estate Superstars,** $69.50 each.
- ☐ **6. Equity Sharing "An Answer for the Eighties,"** $350.00 each.
- ☐ **7. How to Syndicate Single Family Homes,** $69.50 each.

Name _____

Address _____

City/State/Zip _____

Check enclosed ☐   Charge me ☐

Visa # _____   Mastercharge # _____

Expiration Date _____

Signature _____

Total of Your Order _____

Postage (Please add $2.00 for the first
order, and $1.00 for all additional orders) _____

California Residents add 6% sales tax _____

Total _____

HAL MORRIS COMPANIES

175 South Los Robles Avenue, Pasadena, CA; Phone (213) 577-7444